NICOLE ANGELIQU
MPH, RDN, BT

YOU ARE DEATHLESS

A NEAR DEATH EXPERIENCE
TAUGHT ME HOW TO FULLY LIVE
AND NOT FEAR DEATH

ISBN Paperback – # 979-8-9862840-0-2
ISBN Electronic – # 979-8-9862840-1-9

Library of Congress Control Number – # 2022909635

Portions of this book are works of nonfiction. Certain names and identifying characteristics have been changed.

With New Eyes Publishing
Printed in the United States of America.

Nicole Kerr
North Carolina, United States

www.NicoleKerr.com

DEDICATION

To my husband, Paul David Deering,
who saw in me what I could not see in myself,
until one day I could.
I came back and now I know why.

ACKNOWLEDGEMENTS

I am deeply grateful for all the healthcare and medical personnel that have attended to me over the years, and especially at the scene of the accident.

To those in the book industry, especially editors and coaches Michelle Williams and Kristen Wise, and Kristin, Maira, and all the behind-the-scenes personnel at PRESStinely.

To my 'Ohana, especially my husband, Paul, and the unseen Angels, Guides, and Source/God/Creator who helped bring this book into reality – my deepest appreciation and love.

TABLE OF CONTENTS

INTRODUCTION

My True Confession

All of us fear death. That fear remains below the surface of conscious awareness most of the time. Yet, none of us are immune. After all, what is fear if not the body's reaction to the possibility of its own end?

Name any fear. Fear of poverty. Fear of failure. Fear of abandonment. Any you can come up with, I can trace it back to this primal fear of death. The body is a collection of programs, all of them designed for survival. But I fear rejection, you tell me. That's not about dying.

Isn't it, though? As a child, your body very much needed the support of your parents in order to survive. You physically needed their acceptance. On a grander scale, we have needed acceptance in the human tribe for physical survival, too, along with emotional well-being. If you fear rejection, at least part of that fear comes from your body's fear of death.

Eventually all of those programs, however, will one day fail. You will die. The body you inhabit will cease and start decomposing. Why, then, do I make the audacious claim that you are deathless?

Luckily, your physical body serves as just one aspect of who you are, and a small one at that. I know because I've been there, done that. Chief Seattle (Sealth) from the Suquamish tribe summed up my experience beautifully: "There is no death. Only a change of worlds."

Through a near-death experience (NDE), one that I'll describe in more detail later in this book, I've seen the world beyond this one.

Believe me: You have nothing to fear.

Don't get me wrong. I deal with fear, too, all the time. I'm not claiming that I have transcended my body's survival drives, just because, once upon a time, I clinically died. But I have received lots of understanding and inspiration from my NDE. I have been working to integrate and make sense of it in my daily life ever since it happened.

Apparently, I'm not alone. Such events happen more often than you might think: In the U.S., an estimated nine million people have reported an NDE, according to a 2011 study in *Annals of the New York Academy of Sciences*.

No two NDEs take the exact same shape, of course. They vary as widely as any human experience here on earth. Although there is no widely accepted definition of NDEs, according to leading NDE researcher, Dr. Bruce Greyson, the term typically refers to the mystical, profound experiences that people report when they are close to death or experience death. "They're most common in patients who survive severe head trauma or cardiac arrest. In other words, conditions in which you would die, and stay dead, unless somebody instituted emergency medical procedures to help you."

Still, a few common elements weave themselves through all recorded NDE accounts, no matter the culture or religious beliefs people hold. Hence the ten lessons that were identified by the International Association for Near-Death Studies (IANDS). I have listed one of these ten lessons below each chapter title. Dr. Raymond Moody Jr., who coined the term near-death experience in his book, *Life After Life*, shares one of the most consistent features of NDE stories from people around the world: seeing bright light. Here's how he describes it.

> *"What is perhaps the most incredible common element in the accounts I have studied and is certainly the element which has the most profound effect upon the individual, is the encounter with a very bright light. Typically, at its first appearance this light is dim, but it rapidly gets brighter until it reaches an unearthly brilliance. Yet even though this light (usually said to be white or 'clear') is of an indescribable brilliance, many make the specific point that it does not in any way hurt their eyes, or dazzle them, or keep them from seeing other things around them (perhaps because at this point they don't have physical "eyes" to be dazzled)."*

Yup. I could clearly remember the white lights I had encountered when my body flew from the Corvette. When I first read this passage from Dr. Moody's book, I found my head nodding up and down, yes, yes!

Still, I doubted my experience for a long time.

Why?

For one thing, I grew up with strict religious programming. More on that soon. For now, I'll just say, no one in my world had room for the story of my experience beyond my body. Maybe I had just made the whole thing up or imagined it, right?

Also, I eventually was trained as a scientist. I don't need to tell you that mainstream science has invested lots of time and energy into reducing NDEs to the mad hallucinations of a dying brain, combined with the delusional side-effects of religious expectations. On that last count, I can promise nothing I experienced matched the extensive religious expectations of life after death pummeled into me throughout my childhood. And I can no longer stomach the idea that my NDE arose from my body's delusional attempt to hold on to this body and the world it inhabits. When I left my body, I left this world behind. No longer did the drive for survival plague me. Instead of witnessing a desperate attempt to hold on to the world, I experienced a state so delightful that I had no care about whether or not my life continued. In fact, it was continuing.

But in my earlier years, I doubted myself in all things, not just the NDE. The scientists made such convincing arguments. Who was I to go against them?

I will spend the rest of this book answering that question. Along the way, I hope you, too, will find answers. Insights. Understanding of your own relationship to the big stuff like God, the meaning of life, how to live well, and, yes, how to die. I'm talking about your own answers here, not just mine. I don't promise to deliver the five steps to instant happiness or the three easy and simple techniques that will totally revamp your life. In other words, you won't find blogpost copy. No email marketing headlines either, and no pat answers. Just a bit of what I've learned from doing my own dance with death.

Through its pages, this book does make reference to science, especially the science of the brain. When I think it can help you, I share exactly where I got my information. To be honest, though, I know you can Google a lot of this stuff yourself. I have written, not a scientific treatise on death, NDEs or any other topic, but rather an exploration of my own encounter with death and all that it has sparked for me. For that reason, you won't find extensive citations of my sources.

You also won't always find the real names of people. To protect myself and others, I have changed some names where appropriate.

As a child, I witnessed scores of Southern Baptist baptisms. All of them followed a similar script. First, a little speech about the person's commitment to walk a new path, a life with Christ. Then the dunking with the words, "Buried with Him in the likeness of death." When the pastor lifted the new congregant back out of the water, he always said, "Rising to walk in the newness of life."

This book shares my own conversion experience—not in a church, and not by choice. The baptism of the car accident split my life in two. I had my life before the accident. And now I have a second life, the one after the accident. It has followed a trajectory nothing like the one of that first life, and it has dealt me a host of physical challenges I still deal with today. But the emotional and spiritual hurdles that have arisen from the NDE have challenged me in even bigger ways. I have had to raise myself up, out of the not-really-living state of being that I inherited, and into the newness that life itself offers to all of us, all the time.

That's why I often explain that my NDE was a STE: Spiritually Transformative Experience. Over the course of many decades, it has transformed every aspect of my life, from what I eat, to who I married, to how I make my way through a normal day -- not to mention my career. I know for certain that without the crash, I would never have had a life that looks the way mine does now.

And this life, the one I've been building these last four decades since the crash, it's a life I love. For that reason, I feel deep, deep gratitude. In spite of – or maybe because of – the many challenges the crash has created for me, I am grateful for what happened. I am grateful for the many loving people who helped me find my way. And I am grateful, deeply grateful, for the opportunity to share it all with you.

I cherish the hope that you will find this book both useful and effective.

Last photo taken of me prior to the crash. Midday at General Burshnick's, Commandant of Cadets, home with two other 3-degree cadets. We were there to speak with interested high school students about the Academy. You never know when your last picture will be taken.

PRAYER OF PASSING

Know that everything you do and everything you have done has been a contribution to The Whole. Bless-ed be who you are.

When the time comes for your Eternal Spirit to leave this Earthly body...

Your wings will unfurl, the breath of the wind will uplift you, and you will be born anew without effort.

For where you are going there is no pain, no fear, no heartache. There is only love.

You will breathe one last breath while your spirit occupies your physical body, and with the next in-breath you will breathe a breath of great Light. You will feel more love than you have known for a long, long time. For you are going Home.

In the turning of the seasons, the love within your heart, the love of your being has expanded into fullness and now settles in peace to rest.

In the dawn of ages, your spirit has celebrated your essence which, once again, is to be made new.

In the flowing of the rivers, know beyond a doubt of doubts the truth that your spirit is truly one with the Divine Whole.

One Heart... One Mind... One Spirit... One.

You are the blessing. You are the peace. You are the love.

You are the Light within the holiness.

You are the Flight within the freedom.

You are the Essence in the center of the blossom.

This is who you are, and much, much more.

Much, much more.

~Anara Solray
Healing Potentials Unlimited, ©1999

CHAPTER 1: THE CRASH

Lesson 1
We do not "die!" *

1965 Corvette Convertible the day after the crash at the towing lot. Passenger side shown.

* Source: https://mcusercontent.com/6aeb61681f6c311e999fff730/files/5070a118-63b3-4ac3-87f4-08b4f5d6e2e0/2020_IANDS_Annual_Report.01.pdf pg. 15

*"When I hit the ground, I am going to die.
For an instant, one glorious moment that stretches
behind and ahead of me to each horizon, I am suspended,
hovering between heaven and earth like an angel. But I
know it can't last. I am not an angel, and any second now
gravity will have its way with me. I am going to die."*

These were the thoughts going through my head as I flew through the air.

A strange stillness washed over me. Then my soft body crashed into the hard earth below, and I left the known world behind.

Of course, death is not supposed to happen this way. I was only nineteen years old. I still had things to do, places to go, and most importantly, deadlines to meet. My English paper was due on Monday; and I had a quiz in electrical engineering, a subject my brain didn't seem to grasp. Besides all that, I was supposed to be yelling at the new class of doolies (freshman) for screwing up, or for not screwing up, as the case may be. So, I could not be dead. I didn't have time to be dead.

Yet, I think I am. This must be death. Rays of brilliant white light flooded me from all sides. Streams of light cocooned me, wrapping every part of my being in a chrysalis of soothing waves. Instead of the pain of impact, I felt rocked and held. This was bliss.

At the Scene

At 19:20 hours (7:20 p.m.) on the night of August 28, 1983, volunteer paramedic John Hartling was watching TV with his wife and sixteen-year-old son when his phone rang. The dispatcher reported a motor vehicle accident on North Gate Boulevard in Monument, Colorado, with two people involved. John and his son, Pat, immediately jumped in their new sky-blue Ford F-150 pickup truck and floored it to fulfill their duty as first responders.

The first thing John saw at the crash scene was a body, at least what looked like a body, lying under the hood of the car, both about 100 feet from the car itself. Several people had gathered around something in another direction which pulled his attention away from the hood. When he joined them, he understood why they had gathered there.

On the ground, a body lay covered in a blanket. Pulling back the cover, John began questioning the cluster of people around him. Did anyone see the accident? Did they know what happened? A voice above him responded.

"We heard this loud crashing noise and ran to check it out. When we arrived, this girl wasn't moving or breathing so we thought she was dead. Someone got a blanket and covered her up."

John was already working on the victim, checking her vitals, her reflexes, looking for any sign of life. Years of training and experience, together with instinct, made this process second nature, something he could almost do in his sleep. The person above him kept talking.

"Seems like there were two people. The other person is over there, under the hood of the car. So, you might want to go check it out."

John looked up at the group of bystanders. With authority he said, "Listen, nobody tells me what to do. I make the call on life and death decisions, and I don't take the word of bystanders."

But inside John was thinking, "I can see why they thought she was already gone." A quick assessment revealed a young female, unconscious, with a cut from the pelvic area all the way to her right knee. Her left foot appeared amputated, her right wrist was snapped in half, and a clear, fatty tissue, almost like lye, oozed all over from her. Worst of all, there was no blood. With all these injuries, she should be lying in a pool of it. Something was seriously wrong. In all my years as an EMT, if anybody ever looked dead, it certainly is this poor girl."

Finding no pulse, John started with a pain stimulus technique (the sternal knuckle rub) to see if she would respond. He needed some sign of life to keep going with this girl. As he continued to work his knuckles over her sternum, he finally saw the slightest flicker of her right eyelid.

"Well, she isn't gone yet. Maybe we can salvage this."

Behind him, John's partner, Ken Bates, was already working on the person under the hood who was at least conscious.

Minutes later, the Tri Lakes Fire and Ambulance Department roared onto the scene.

Frantically, John and the EMTs worked on the girl: hooking her up to an oxygen mask, fumbling for a vein in her neck where they finally sank an IV, and getting the anti-shock trousers over her legs to squeeze blood back up to her heart. These pants were cutting-edge stuff, so new that John had barely completed training on them. But he knew getting them on her was probably the single biggest thing he could do to keep her alive. It was the toughest thing about this job, having someone's life depend on your first try at something like this.

On the count of three, the group lifted the girl onto the gurney, slid her into the ambulance, and slammed the door shut. The ambulance raced away, sirens blazing, into the darkening evening.

Inside the ambulance, Ken and John were trying to keep their victim alive. For the entire ride to the hospital, they gave her CPR. Still, the girl's blood pressure was just 60/0; her vitals were catastrophically low. Things looked grim.

By the time the ambulance pulled into the emergency room (ER) bay at Penrose Community Hospital, Dr. Amilu Stewart was running down the corridor to meet the EMTs. She had gotten the call at 19:45 hours (7:45 p.m.), near the end of dinner. A serious case, she needed to get to Penrose STAT the voice on the other line had barked. Even with ten years as a trauma surgeon under her belt, Dr. Stewart had not gotten used to these calls. She wondered if she ever would.

Now she stood over the victim. One look told her the girl was in very bad shape. I don't know if she is going to make it, she admitted to herself, no matter what I do.

Beyond

I was floating. The world behind me, my life as a Cadet in the United States Air Force Academy, my classes, all the papers, all the responsibilities—it's all faded, now a vague and distant memory. The light around me was everything. It's a river and all I had to do was let it carry me.

This is a good place, a safe place; I knew it. A place without pain. Like a cloud, I glided upward, still immersed in light. I was completely weightless, an astronaut in outer space. A high like I never dreamed possible.

Meanwhile...

State Trooper Ken Raczkowski got the call about this gruesome scene at 19:28 hours (7:28 p.m.). When he arrived just ten minutes later the Black Forest Ambulance Service, Tri-Lakes Fire and Rescue, and the El Paso Fire Department were already there. But without talking to any of them, he knew. He knew before even parking the car. This was a bad one.

Standing on the shoulder beside his parked car, he surveyed the wreckage of what had once been a Corvette. The driver was still there, one Nate Smith. Trooper Raczkowski watched as Nate resisted the efforts of emergency personnel to assist him. The trooper only spoke briefly with the boy—was he nineteen, twenty?—but the odor of alcohol on his breath had been impossible to miss. Since no one had seen the accident, Raczkowski would have to put two and two together to make sense of this mess.

Eventually he would report a one car accident involving a two door 1965 Chevrolet Corvette with two occupants. Cadet N. Smith had been driving the vehicle westbound on North Gate Boulevard at an estimated speed of 70 mph in a 45-mph zone. The driver lost control on a curve to the left, causing his car to spin off to the right. Leading with the right side, the car continued for 124 feet where it then struck a large boulder on the passenger side. Impact threw the boulder twenty feet, and the vehicle continued for another twenty-eight feet after collision. It flipped onto its top, where it came to rest facing west. Both parties were ejected from the vehicle, the driver landing partially under the hood and the passenger falling just east of the boulder in a ditch. The occupant thrown clear was unconscious and could not give a statement.

This person was subsequently identified as Nicole Angelique Kerr.

Back at Penrose, it was turning into a very long night for Dr. Stewart. Technically, the girl was dead. But the doctor refused to give up. Not yet. In the operating room, under the doctor's direction the surgical team resuscitated the girl repeatedly over the next couple of hours. They pumped fluids and blood into the body, straining to coax vital signs from the thin, limp frame on their table. But she wasn't stabilizing. If this kid was going to make it, she had to stabilize.

Then, out of nowhere, she suddenly did. What had happened? Dr. Stewart couldn't say. Only that the girl had somehow come back. Her vitals were stable. Now began the tedious process of cleaning her up. Pavement, fiberglass, car paint, grass, feces, dirt, debris—the accident had ground all of it and more into the wounds and gashes that pitted her body. And there was the matter of the girl's left foot. They would have to put it back on. That would require a specialist. Come to think of it, this girl was going to need a whole lot of specialists.

Dr. Stewart left the hospital the next morning completely spent. Only a short paragraph of notes, jotted before she headed home, would mark the details of the ordeal she herself had just endured. But she had saved the girl's life. It was worth it.

Back to Life

The following months of my life passed not at the Academy, driven by papers and pushups, but in a hospital room, hemmed in by the beeping of monitors, the in-and-out traffic of strangers dressed in scrubs. Someone close by would always be checking on this or that vital sign, giving me yet another medication, or talking with my mother in low tones. My father was there, too. Even when I couldn't see him, I could sense his six-foot two-inch frame hovering over me. "Colie, Colie can you hear me?" his commanding voice called to me. "You are a fighter, girl. All the Kerrs are. And you are a winner."

Eventually that voice, and not the voice of an angel, would be the one I would tune myself to once again. Whatever had happened to me in that place beyond death, I shoved into the darkest reaches of my awareness. Out of sight, yes, but not entirely out of mind.

Many years later I would interview the EMT who saved my life, as well as the doctor and the nurse. Only then did I really begin to let myself own what had happened to me. Since it happened, I knew I had fought to survive. What began to re-emerge, though, was the beautiful, powerful experience of a love and healing I had encountered at death.

If death is an end, then I know for certain there is nothing final about it.

Two Cadets Injured

RESCUE WORKERS aided two U.S. Air Force Cadets who were seriously injured Sunday, August 28, when their car skidded off Northgate Road for 171 feet, hit a boulder and moved it 20 feet. The car continued for another 28 feet, overturning once and coming to

Newspaper report of crash on September 1, 1983. EMT John Harting, EMT Ken Bates, Pat Hartling plus fire department crew working on Nicole.

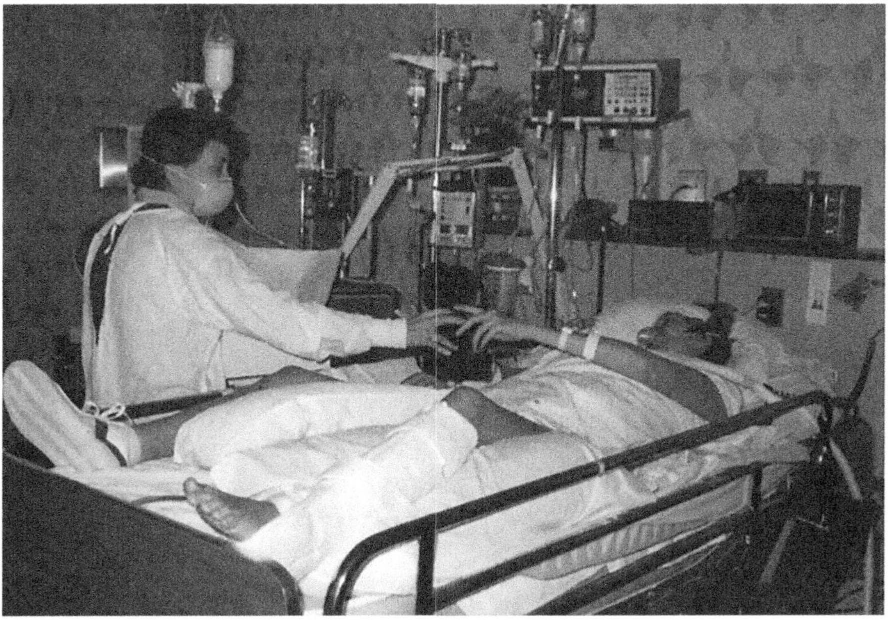

This is the first photo taken of me in the ICU of Penrose Community Hospital, approximately four weeks after the crash. I am with my high school friend, Shannon Dortch.

CHAPTER 2: THE DIE IS CAST

Lesson 2:
Be grateful: the Universe is working in your favor.

How did I wind up as a cadet in the U.S. Air Force Academy? What would possess a girly-gal from the deep south who enjoyed modeling (on the teen board called Gayfer Girls), extra-curricular activities like Junior Achievement (a business entrepreneurship program), ballet, writing, and soft sports like softball and racquetball to choose such a life path? The answer is simple, to please my father.

As a graduate of the class of 1960, he was delighted with the government's decision in 1976 to admit women to the military academies. My dad always wanted one of his four children to carry on the family legacy, so I stepped up for the assignment. Yes, sir!

I have two younger brothers, James and Sean, who also did time serving in the military when they were young, around fourteen years old, at the Marine Military Academy in Harlingen, Texas. My dad's heavy-handed persuasion once again. They both wound up going to "regular" universities. While in my junior year of high school, the only colleges I even considered were the U.S. military academies. Some people my age sought personal accomplishment. But for me, what better level of accomplishment could I attain than to gain the Kerr stamp of approval? I aimed for admittance into my dad's alma mater, the United States Air Force Academy (USAFA). I was going to be "his boy" after all, even if it killed me.

If you've ever been to Colorado Springs, Colorado, you have probably visited the impressive USAFA. This popular tourist attraction sits in the foothills of the majestic Rocky Mountains. It is a sister school to the United States Naval Academy in Annapolis, Maryland, and West Point, in Hudson, New York. If you can survive four years in any of these institutions, you receive a Bachelor of Science degree and your commission in the respective branch of service. For the Air Force, I would become a second lieutenant.

Getting accepted into one of the service academies practically takes an act of Congress. Kidding aside, I had to garner a congressional nomination just to apply. (Thank you, Representative Wayne Dowdy - Mississippi!) I also underwent medical and physical fitness exams, gathered multiple letters of recommendations, and pushed myself to score high on the ACT. If I'm honest, on some level I didn't believe I would make it through all these hurdles to gain admission. But in April of 1982, the principal of my high school called me into his office to inform me of my acceptance into the class of 1986, only the sixth class of women to attend.

I was stunned.

My friends would soon find themselves at Ole Miss or Mississippi State University in the normal college scene. I, on the other hand, was heading to boot camp. What had I done?

There was no going back. I had to go.

Get in Line, Soldier

I arrived at the Academy June 28, 1982, and the next six weeks, known as basic cadet training (BCT), were pure hell for me. I was not a varsity athlete. Sure, I did lots of physical activities in high school -- softball, racquetball, and dance, like ballet and drill team. Think NYC Rockettes, not ROTC. None of that had prepared me for boot camp. When I found out I was accepted into the Academy, I had put myself on a "run around the block in combat boots" program of my own invention. Mind you, this I did in Jackson, Mississippi, at sea level. Colorado Springs sits 7,000 ft. above sea level.

I almost passed out during the first BCT run. I wound up at the back of the group and stayed there for the rest of the six weeks of boot camp. I fell so far behind the others, they sent me to remedial training known as R- Flight, a one-on-one intense training program. I was praying just to survive.

Despite vicious hazing and a culture of sexual harassment and abuse, I was keeping my nose down and chin in at the Air Force Academy. I did everything I could to convince myself I was happy. After all, my parents sure were.

CHAPTER 3: WHO AM I?

Lesson 3: *Love is all that matters and is the source of all that exists.**

The Academy: Day 1

I showed up on a sunny day in late June 1982 sporting a hip, short haircut with my new bag of Estee Lauder cosmetics and several new fashionable outfits in tow. My goodbyes to my family went on for a while, but I knew my moment had come. I confidently walked up the "Bring Me Men" ramp (the words have since been changed) as it was time to start my new life at the Air Force Academy.

As I joined the line to be "processed in," upperclassmen were yelling at me. They promptly took my suitcase, the one with all my worldly possessions, including my treasured cosmetics and new wardrobe. "You won't need them!" they insisted. Protest was useless.

They even took my contact lenses, issuing me black-rimmed square glasses, affectionately called "b.c. glasses," short for birth control. I soon discovered how well they worked, too. When you wear them, nobody will want to look at you, much less have sex.

As I made my way down the line, I was given several types of military uniforms (dress blues, camos, etc.) and issued everything except bras. When I got to my "dorm" room, I dumped all my clothes on a metal-framed twin bed. I fished my new underwear out of the pile and shrieked. It had elastic in the waist, but not in the leg holes! Yes, granny britches! When I retrieved my royal blue one-piece swimsuit, I found it had a cute skirt attached. Not bad, but a world away from the itsy-bitsy Speedos the guys were issued. Since I am tall (5' 11") and long-legged, they issued me men's pants and women's tops. All too soon the misfortune of this gender mismatch hit hard.

* Source: https://mcusercontent.com/6aeb61681f6c311e999fff730/files/5070a118-63b3-4ac3-87f4-08b4f5d6e2e0/2020_IANDS_Annual_Report.01.pdf pg. 15

My clothes never lined up right for the "gig line" inspection because men's shirts button right-to-left and women's, vice versa. I accrued many demerits since I was not allowed to explain my so-called "mistake." I also found in the pile, men's white, V-neck t-shirts for physical education. I discovered the fun when I found myself doing pushups with the upperclassmen, which we did face to face. With those V-necks, the men looked right down my shirt and saw – well, my bra and boobs.

Even though I had my beautiful long, blonde hair cut off before I entered the Academy, I discovered I hadn't gone far enough. Off to the barber shop I went with the rest of my squadron. The lone "beautician" proceeded to give me and every other woman the same "Dorothy Hamill" haircut. Better than the buzz cut the men were receiving, but not flattering on me. I looked like I was wearing a soup bowl.

Finally, Parents' Weekend arrived. It marked the transition from BCT to becoming a fourth classmen or "doolie." The approximately 1,400 of us who have just made it through BCT could now count ourselves as part of the cadet wing.

With my family supervising, I was allowed to leave the Academy for the weekend. My first break in six weeks. I headed straight to the Regis Salon in the local mall to have my haircut corrected. That handled, I took the only logical next step. I ordered a thick and chewy Supreme at Pizza Hut.

How did I get here?

At this point in my life, I was not doing anything differently from my normal. Yes, the details now looked a lot different. Instead of using my spare time to socialize with church friends over sweet tea, I was huffing my way through endless hours of grueling physical training, not to mention putting up with demeaning insults and sexual innuendo constantly directed my way.

But underneath all that? I was still just pleasing my father. Same as I had been doing for as long as I could remember. More than anything else... more than the makeup I loved, or the chit chat I had enjoyed with my girlfriends, more than the good grades I got in school, or the good looks I so carefully cultivated... I cared about this. I was a good girl, my father's daughter. I had built my whole identity around it.

How did that happen?

In our family, my father rigidly enforced a strict code of conduct. The severest penalty I can remember came in elementary school when my siblings and I were sentenced to a summer of no TV. None. For the full three months. All because we did not shut up in the car when we were told to do so. It registered as the worst summer on record for all of us. I felt beyond crushed to miss *The Six Million Dollar Man* and *The Miss America Pageant*. But even when we didn't receive a punishment like this one, we all knew that a minor misstep would likely result in an unhappy encounter with "Billy," my father's name for the big, black belt he used to whip us.

Under my father's leadership, we lived not only with God's Ten Commandments, but we also had to abide by his Ten Commandments. Being a military man, he had lots of experience with making sure those below him followed orders. We knew breaking his Commandments would mean harsh consequences.

So, here they are; my dad's Ten Commandments:

1. **No spending the night. Ever.** His rationale was that nothing productive ever came from it. Kids staying up most of the night, then cranky and tired the next day. No, not his kids.
2. **Make sure you are in the house by 8:00 p.m.** Except if you were at work, school, or a church function.
3. **No alcohol allowed in the house and no drinking alcohol. Ever.** He was raised by an alcoholic father and knew all too well how much alcohol could harm a person and a family. My mom is Ukrainian-German, and he even threw out the sherry she used for cooking. To his credit, he is no hypocrite about this one. I have never seen him drink alcohol or pay for it at dinner, even at our weddings.
4. **Work always comes before fun.** We had chores assigned in addition to Mom's expectations of keeping our room neat and tidy at all times. Saturdays were chore days. Normally we spent all day doing them. Before we could have our $2.50 per week allowances, the chore list had to pass inspection by our mother, whose standards registered off the charts. By 4:00 p.m., we might get the reward of going swimming at a local hotel swimming pool with pizza to follow. But not always. The reward was never a given.
5. **You WILL do what I say because I know what is best for you. I better not have to repeat myself.**

6. **Attend church on Sundays, both morning and evening services. No excuses. You will sit with me in church, not with friends. And you will stay awake.**
7. **Transportation needed? Ride your bike if you want to go somewhere.** We learned how to ride banana-seat bikes in the parking lot of Jitney Jungle grocery store. Dad told me to get on the bike, proceeded to push me off, and well, over I went. No bike helmets, no knee pads, no nothing. Just me, my bike, and the concrete pavement. Ouch, indeed.
8. **Do not go in and out of the house while the air conditioner is running. You are wasting money.**
9. **Prepare to be punished if you did something wrong.** As we got older, we hated most the punishment of having our phone privileges revoked. We shared just one push-button phone, mounted to the wall in the kitchen with a long cord on it.
10. **No smoking or doing drugs. And for that matter, no dating.**

Throughout my childhood and into early adulthood, I can remember consciously breaking his commandments only two times. Here is the first one, an incident from the fourth grade involving commandments 1, 5, and 9.

Criminal Activity

I didn't get invited to many sleep overs. So, for my best friend Leigh Ann Burns to have her birthday party as a sleep over—well, I just HAD to go.

Game plan: plead and beg Mom for weeks leading up to the event. Leigh Ann's birthday and mine are both during the first week of February. That year, the only thing I asked for as a present was to go to Leigh Ann's sleepover. Mom knew her mom, Carolyn, well since we lived in the same neighborhood. It's not like I was headed to some house full of immoral parents with wild and crazy teenagers lurking around corners. I thought I might have a chance.

Finally, Mom gave in. I could go. And—she informed me on the next breath—she was going to be in big trouble with my father for doing this. Just so I knew. Geez, hearing that, was like all the fun was gone already, and I was not there yet.

But I went anyway. How could I not? Finally, I would find out why everyone made such a big deal about spend-the-night parties. We played party games and told scary stories. Her dad even got in on the fun by dressing up as a spooky person. He sent all of us girls screaming through their house.

I tried my best to enjoy the night. All this should be fun. But, honestly, the thought of going home the next morning and facing my father never strayed far from my mind.

Back home, his anger met me at the front door. Before I stepped inside the lectures had already started. He hoped I enjoyed it. Because this was the last time it was going to happen. And I was now grounded for two weeks instead of getting a whipping. Also, my mother was in trouble, whatever that meant. Plus, I had to start all my Saturday chores right then. No rest allowed.

After this I would never spend the night with friends. Not ever. Well, not until I met my roommates, Margaret, Sharon, and Lori at the USAFA at age eighteen.

Lesson Learned

My dad's rules—and the heavy-handed way he enforced them—taught me early on that I would need to please him to survive. Long ago I had learned to suppress my own desires and even joys to fit what he required from me. From a young age, I developed the habit of telling myself it was what I wanted most. Who was I anyway? Without being my father's daughter, I was pretty much nobody.

No surprise, then, that I found myself grinning and bearing at the Air Force Academy.

Who am I?

I'm not sure I could have made it through my childhood without learning to sacrifice my own needs to please my parents. In fact, the strategy worked so well with them that I ended up doing it with everyone. Teachers, relatives, friends, strangers. If everyone else was happy, then I was happy.

Or was I? Eventually, I discovered the identity of "people pleaser" to be my Achilles' heel. Little did I know that with the excavation of my identity as a people pleaser, I was uncovering a root cause of so many things that didn't work in my life, one that was set in motion long before I realized I was even doing it. The discovery set off a landslide for me.

Of course, back in my days as a cadet at the AFA, I did not know the term "people pleaser." Heck, I didn't even understand the word "identity." If someone had asked me to describe it, I would have had no words at all. In more recent times, the word "identity" often gets paired with the word "politics." These two in combination tend to divide and polarize.

So, I feel the need to define the word "identity" in terms of how I'm using it in this book. I'm referring to the way you think about who you are. This kind of identity shapes your internal landscape. Also, you don't have just one identity but many identities. You may or may not talk to others about a particular identity you carry. But certainly, you act from it. I'm not talking about political rallies, either. I'm referring to the kind of actions you take in everyday moments when you're not thinking about your identity.

Identity in this sense includes a conception of yourself that evolves over the course of your life. Things you have no control over—your gender, ethnicity, upbringing, culture—all play into it. It also has roots in things you decide, your beliefs, choices, preferences. You create and recreate your identity from a collection of constantly changing parts: Your physical body, mind, emotions, circumstances.

To make some sense of it, consider that you develop some core identities pretty early on in life...

Born a Disappointment

I was born a big baby. A whopping 10.5 pounds! And my father refused to believe the nurse's proclamation: "Congrats! You have a healthy baby... girl." He literally had to lift the diaper himself to receive confirmation of the disappointing news. At that weight, he was expecting the next linebacker for the Dallas Cowboys.

Would you believe me if I told you that I sensed in utero that my parents wanted a boy? It might sound far-fetched to you, or maybe you can relate. Science supports the idea now, showing that the state of the mother directly affects the state of her child. Science or not, I know I felt, before even coming into the world, that I was going to be a big letdown.

Before you were born, you came up against expectations, too. We all did. At age zero you're already getting set up for some of the core identities you'll adopt. My own core pattern of people pleasing began when I knew I was not what my parents were hoping for. I was going to have to work extra hard to get their approval. And, boy, did I.

My over-concern for others at my own expense drove me through life. I would say "I'm sorry" all the time. Having anyone upset with me made me extremely uncomfortable. It follows that I had a difficult time saying no. And conflict? My anxiety levels would shoot through the roof. I avoided it at all costs. Admitting to another person when I felt hurt by their actions—especially if that person was my mother—felt almost impossible to me.

To be clear, people pleasing is not about being kind or even nice. My eagerness to please actually stemmed from a low sense of self-worth. To feel good, I needed someone to praise me. I pretzeled myself into any shape I could to get that praise. The whole time I had no idea how little I regarded myself.

As a girl born and raised in the south, I had slipped on this identity like a second skin. I could not even tell I was wearing it. But it was having an impact on me. I like to say that people pleasing is just as innocuous as drinking lots of sweet tea. Down south, that sweet tea comes with every meal, and at least a few times a day in between. As pleasant as it tastes, we know that consuming vast quantities of refined sugar causes diabetes, obesity, inflammation, and other health problems. The same thing happens with people pleasing. Eventually you end up with dis-ease in your body, most notably, stomach and gallbladder issues (2001 N.E.T., Inc Master Chart).

All my efforts to please my parents, to gain recognition that would prove something to them—especially my father—never worked. No amount of achievement could ever replace what I really wanted: love and approval from myself.

In the grab bag of identity, your own core identities may not match mine at all. Instead of a people pleaser, you might have styled yourself into a James Dean protégé, the perpetual rebel with (or without) a cause. Works great until you realize how much you push other people away and live with loneliness. Or you might have become the consummate peacemaker, someone who takes pride in helping everyone get along. Aren't you so good? Oh, except, you never experience authenticity in your relationships because you don't ever want to make waves. (I'll admit that one rings true for me, too.) Maybe you're the truth teller. No one in your family ever wanted to face the facts or admit their real feelings, so you made it your job to feel all the feelings everyone else avoided and call everyone on the carpet. Now you don't really know when words are better left unsaid. If that fits you, then you probably don't understand why a lot of people don't like you. Unlike you, they don't want to hurt your feelings by saying it to your face.

Your Legacy

I have shared how my identity as a people pleaser was set in motion in the womb. Actually, though, I'm confident it started even before that. Ever hear the old story about the woman who always cut off the ends of her roast before putting it in the pan to bake? When her husband asked her why, she said, "That's how my mother taught me." They visited her mother for the holidays, and he asked her mother why. "That's how my mother taught me," she repeated. Later that day, they visited the woman's grandmother in the nursing home. "Well," the elder explained, "my pan was too small. That was the only way I could get it to fit." How your parents and/or step-parents raised you is strongly influenced by how their parents raised them, and so on down the line—even if it doesn't make sense anymore. Generational patterning becomes entrenched.

How you communicate with others—or choose not to. How you hold or express emotions. How you ask for and get your needs met (or not). Your self-image, your worldview. Is the world safe or unsafe? Can you trust women? Men? Relationships? These and a host of other coping strategies are learned in our families of origin. Raising kids can be a stressful business. Despite their best intentions, most parents unconsciously fall back on patterns they learned from their own parents, whether the patterns work or not. Most families pass down generations of dysfunction along with the heirloom china. This dysfunction, as well as a host of other positive and neutral aspects of your experience, are woven into your identity. Identities, really. Unconscious of their presence most of the time, you think of these identities as just "me."

Your body also anchors all these identities. Essentially, the body wants to stay in homeostasis. It acts as the lynchpin that keeps everything in place.

Who am I—really?

When I left my body during the accident, I encountered a whole new identity. I was not a daughter. Not a student with a pile of homework that had to be done. Not even a people pleaser. Heck, I wasn't even a girl named Nicole.

I was something more, so much more than all this. Something that did not change with my body, my hair color, my test scores. Something that could not be touched by my mother's guilt trips or my father's stern opinion. I was an individual consciousness, yes, but one beyond all identities.

In that world without identities, I learned that I am deathless.

Swiftly, though, I buried that awareness when I returned to my body on this side of the veil. As Nicole, I had very little in my world to help me make sense of the experience. Naturally, I locked it away along with all the other square-shaped things about myself that I could not fit into the decidedly round holes of my life.

That's why the notion of identity figures so strongly in my story. For years I would struggle to make sense of the dichotomy between the total freedom I experienced beyond my body, without a notion of identity, versus my seemingly unavoidable need for limiting identities to survive the world I lived in here. What did death have to teach me about who I really was?

For starters, I cannot explain away the fact that all my identities would someday come to an end. Full stop. I had already gone there, to the realm of the dead, which made the denial of it impossible.

This existence beyond identity explains, in part, why death scares us so much. After all, who are we without a name, a face, a race, a creed? Without career achievements, roles like motherhood or teacher or business owner, the status of money or the comfort of family? Do we even exist without those things?

What I learned was, yes, an emphatic YES! On the other side of death, I was still very much a self. An individual consciousness, with my own awareness and sense of being. And without the encumbrance of those many identities—name, face, race, etc.—I experienced a freedom and joy I never had before as "Nicole," one I still cannot adequately put into words. To say it another way, life without identity turns out to be pure bliss.

At the same time, life here, in a body and on this planet, actually requires that you function with identity. When it's healthy, identity supports you to fulfill your sense of purpose. When unhealthy, it traps and stymies you.

Which brings me to the distinction between healthy and unhealthy identity. Within the bounds of a healthy identity, you can see yourself through many different external lenses. Wife, daughter, mother, father, American, Brazilian, baseball lover, ballerina, etc. All of these outwardly oriented aspects of identity you hold loosely, though, the way you might approach a night out with close friends. You don't know exactly how all of it will go, but you've known these people for a long time. You don't worry too much about impressions or what might happen; it's a relaxed evening ahead. Tomorrow morning you'll probably have some new memories.

In other words, your identities become healthy through the ways you relate to them. You build a healthy identity when you learn to live from the inside out.

One way to know you are living from a healthy identity is whether or not you remain loyal to your own core needs and callings. Inside of a healthy relationship to your identities, you follow the whispers of your heart and soul, even if the outside world does not agree with your choices. Self-esteem, self-love, and self-care show up in someone with a healthy sense of self.

In case this sounds daunting, you can find comfort in knowing you don't arrive at, once and for all, a healthy relationship with all your identities. Healthy identity is something you do, day to day, moment to moment. Awareness helps the process along, showing you the places where you still cling tightly to an identification. In my own life, I work with my identities all the time.

And if you're anything like me, you may have to spend time learning to hear yourself first. To follow your heart, you have to know what it's saying to you. A regular practice of meditation and stillness can greatly help this along. Journaling also works wonders. The more time you spend with your own mind, the more you will recognize and understand the identities you cling to, despite the fact that they are not your truest, deathless self. Though it can feel arduous sometimes, this work helps you develop a healthy relationship with your identities.

Unhealthy identity, on the other hand, beckons from every street corner. It comes from the external aspects of self that you attach to strongly in order to create a false sense of security. This partly explains why Buddhism encourages us to remain unattached to the outside world. Eventually your identifications with what you see around you will be revealed, in one way or another, for what they really are, coping strategies destined to fail you.

That's because an unhealthy sense of identity, the kind that nearly all of us fall into at least some of the time, centers around the approval of other people. What would your mother say? Wow, wouldn't your brother be jealous right now? Oh, your husband would not approve of this. And, by the way, what awards have you won lately? What's your relationship status, and how good does it look on Instagram? Who calls you, and how "important" are those people?

Know that negative answers to these questions can also point to identities you've latched onto unconsciously. I'm not in a relationship because I'm a loser. I never win awards because I'm stupid. I'm not good enough.

All these identifications come from the part of you that wants safety and security in and for your physical body, even the negative ones.

The voice is the part of you that does not, however, understand how to guide you in creating true fulfillment in your life.

In our culture, we place a lot of emphasis on our work roles. At a party in the States, the first question someone asks after your name is nearly always, "What do you do?" Is it any wonder, then, that so many people die soon after retirement? You can become so over-identified with a role that without it you have no reason to live.

In my case, the behavior of pleasing other people was not, in and of itself, a negative thing. My strong attachment to it made it problematic. I could not bear to see myself, or let others see me, in any other way than pleasing and successful. I became so invested in that identity that I now view it as an addiction.

Any identity, no matter how positive, can turn against you if it's something you "have to" do/be/have. Consider that your attachment to an unhealthy identity could be making you sick. Without it, you might feel lost for a while. Until you realize how much better—lighter, freer, happier—you feel without it

CHAPTER 4: WHO IS GOD?

Lesson 4: *Everything and everyone is connected.**

Where am I?

My mouth was dry. So dry. I woke up, and that's all I could feel. How badly I wanted a drink. Mountain Dew, somebody bring me a Mountain Dew!

"Where am I?" I ask. My voice is a mouse's voice. But I am not a mouse. I am not a human either. Somehow, I have become a pain zombie. Everything everywhere hurts.

"You're in the Intensive Care Unit (ICU) at Penrose Community Hospital," an imposing man tells me. It takes me a moment to realize it's Captain Spencer, my Air Officer Commander. My eyes slide over the details of the room, working to catch up with what he's said.

"What happened?" I finally asked.

"You and Nate were on your way back to the Academy when his car crashed. You were found unconscious and brought here," Captain Spencer tells me with a grave look on his face.

In my mother's world, this is the moment where I wondered if I remembered to put on clean underwear. But I was not thinking of underwear. I was thinking of only one thing, in fact. The one thing I must think about, always.

"Please don't tell my father," I squeak.

"He is going to kill me when he finds out," I thought to myself.

---

* Source: https://mcusercontent.com/6aeb61681f6c311e999fff730/files/5070a118-63b3-4ac3-87f4-08b4f5d6e2e0/2020_IANDS_Annual_Report.01.pdf pg. 15

Since Leigh Ann's slumber party in the fourth grade, I had never again consciously disobeyed him. Until now.

Yesterday...

I was getting ready to leave the squadron softball game at Black Forest Park when I caught the eye of a senior cadet, Nate.

"Hey, can I have a ride back to the Academy with you?" I asked.

"Sure," he answered.

But it took a while for the ride to manifest. We were the last ones to leave the game. On the way home Nate wanted to stop at a bar for another beer.

I'm cool with that, I told myself. So cool, in fact, that I had two beers myself—oh, and a cigarette for good measure. A serious violation of my Father's Ten Commandments. Numbers 3 (no drinking) and 10 (no smoking ... and was this a date, too?). Of course, Number 3 was one of his most important so those two beers might count as breaking more than one Commandment—not to mention the most alcohol I'd ever had in my life.

As we were leaving the bar, I heard the bartender call out to Nate. "Hey, buddy, are you okay to drive?"

Nate nodded. "Yes."

I scrambled into the passenger seat of his red convertible Corvette and kicked back my seat. Soon we were snaking through the winding mountain roads.

Now Nate was pulling over. He wanted to watch the sun set against the Rockies. Was it beautiful? Yes. But I was having a hard time enjoying it. Commandment 4, "Work always comes before fun," kept getting in the way. All I could think about was meeting our 7:35 p.m. curfew. I didn't want to start this new year in trouble. I had received demerits, tours (marching on the weekend from point A to B with your rifle), and confinements (sitting at your desk studying with your door open for hours) my first year and was determined not to do that again my second (3rd degree) year.

Finally, Nate's key was turning in the ignition. His car was pulling back onto the road and heading for the North Gate entrance to the Academy.

Back at the I.C.U.

That's it. All I can remember.

It's enough, though. I know if I don't die from my injuries, my father may well take a crack at me.

Cadet First Class Troy Dixon, my Squadron Commander, informs me they have already called my parents who will be arriving in the next day or so.

I am in too much pain to move, even to a wince. But on the inside, I am cringing.

Then the med cocktail of morphine, valium, and demerol kicks in and I begin to fade.

A Little Backstory

Church. While growing up, the thing I liked the least about it?

Well, there was just so much of it.

Growing up in Mississippi, part of the Bible Belt, meant that church formed a cornerstone of the culture at large. It was a big deal for everyone. On top of that, my family was double dipping. My mom was Lutheran and my dad, Southern Baptist. That meant I went to two different churches every Sunday.

Mornings I usually spent at Christ Lutheran Church for Sunday School and the service, a good three hours. Christ Lutheran had about 100-125 members at most. Eventually I went through confirmation classes there, studying *Luther's Small Catechism* (*Der Kleine Katechismus*) published in 1529.

Sunday evenings I went to Broadmoor Baptist Church, which boasted a membership of hundreds (or even thousands?). I got yet more Bible instruction in the Training Union and Bible Drill. The Training Union taught us all about the church's history and doctrines. During Bible Drill we took turns standing at the front of the room in pairs, then as a group. Our teachers might ask us to quote a specific Bible verse from memory. Or an adult would call out the location of a passage from the Bible, chapter, and verse, then holler, "Go." That gave permission to begin heatedly rifling through our Bibles to find the passage and step out of line acknowledging we found it. Whoever first found the verse correctly, had to recite it, thus receiving a point. The adults called this "sword drilling," since the Bible was the "sword of the Lord." We kids took these competitions seriously, too. To this day I still remember the books of the Bible in order and certain scriptures we had to memorize. Before a Sunday evening had ended, we had to attend another hour-plus-long church service with the adults on top of the Training Union we had already endured.

At least we usually got a fast-food dinner at either Wendy's or McDonald's afterwards.

During our elementary school years, we also went to Wednesday night church meetings at Broadmoor. No such thing as too much! We kids took part in the Royal Ambassador and Girls in Action programs. Here we learned about international Southern Baptist missionaries. All I remember now? The free dinner.

Along with all the services and training programs, the Baptist church boasted a full-size gym, bowling alley, snack shop, and all kinds of organized team sports, including tournaments with gold trophies for the winners. Churches competed against each other, and it was full on. They even had a Minister of Recreation, John Bewely—who was amazing. (Seriously, he was a magician.) He also organized things like Friday night roller skating for us kids. Along with roller skating, I learned from the Baptists how to play softball. And how to "not dance" which is more how to mimic the dancing women on TV or the girls at school who were allowed to dance. Without crossing the line, of course, into, say, touching a boy while we did it, or perhaps, looking like we'd learned any specific series of steps. After all, dancing constituted a sin against the Lord. What we were doing did look an awful lot like dancing, but we would never go so far as to call it that. A rose by any other name?

I have to hand it to the Southern Baptists. They know how to market themselves. Clearly, they had more money than the Lutherans, more people, more resources, and more fun—meaning the rec center, not hell, fire, and brimstone. Around sixth grade we were given a choice between the two. Both my sister and I picked the Lutherans despite their more somber path to heaven. We were actually picking Mom, of course. My brothers went the Baptist way with Dad.

In church I got the message that God dwelt in the gorgeous, blue sky up above, full of fluffy white clouds. Heaven. He looked like a nice old white man with a beard and a kindly face. The Devil, on the other hand, had horns and a pitchfork he would use to skewer you. The Devil lived in Hell, a word we were not allowed to say, except sometimes in church the Baptist preacher said it many times. Hell existed so far down underground that it literally burned. A ceaseless inferno, in fact If you were "bad," an unforgiven sinner, you were going to Hell.

But wait. How could you, a human, stay alive in Hell? I mean, fire burns you up. How could you exist there without being consumed? Wouldn't you turn to ashes pretty quickly? Then what? I tried hard to picture it, especially since I heard it mentioned so often. I prayed the sinner's prayer and watched my brothers get baptized in both churches. I hoped my infant baptism at the Lutheran Church and Confirmation in the 8th grade was good enough. Still, I worried I might end up down in "H-E-double-hockey-sticks" by some mistake. That place was dark. Its only light came from the ever-present flames all around you. If you landed there, then you had only eternal damnation and separation from the rest of your family and friends ahead of you. (Apparently all of your friends and family were good.) No showers or water down there? Do you eat dinner every night with other bad people? And does the Devil serve only barbecue?

So much of what I learned in church didn't make sense to me. Going to two different churches didn't help, either. Both talked about God. But their rules, ceremonies, and interpretations of the Bible differed so much. For instance, the Lutheran church baptizes you as an infant with a sprinkling of water. But the Baptists wait until you're older, a child or adult, then dunk you backwards in a tank of water as deep as a swimming pool. Incidentally, that always formed the most entertaining part of a Baptist service. I loved watching people in their Sunday best walk into water up to their chests. After the pastor put them under, they came up sopping wet. Oh, and "saved." It was nothing like the Lutheran approach, in tone or philosophy. Still, they claimed their way was the right one—just like the Lutherans did. Both churches, I was told again and again by each, had the one right way to God.

Okay, somebody had to be wrong here. Mixing the two religions left me with the impression that even God could get a little confused about what He supposedly said.

Of course, some things did come through loud and clear. Both churches taught me not to question authority. If something they said didn't make sense, then the problem had to lie with me.

I also learned that God was external, meaning, separate from me. He did love me. Yet somehow His main job was to judge and punish me. If I broke the rules, I had sinned. God would get me for it. And I was taught to fear God's ire above all else. I could wind up in Hell for eternity, after all. (Whatever that looked like. See above.) In essence, I had an earthly father and a heavenly father. I'm pretty sure my experience of my own authoritarian father had a strong influence on the version of God I internalized.

What I did not learn at either church was how to have a personal relationship with God. I had many rote prayers to say every day. God called the shots on everything else.

Commandment 9: Prepare to be punished if you did something wrong.

"You brought this on yourself, Nicole."

That's my father speaking. I've just barely survived seven weeks in the ICU, and I've finally been transferred to the pediatric ward. But I haven't seen my father much. He would take off from work and fly in from Mississippi when I was going to have surgery. Apparently, he took one look at my injuries in the early days and fainted from all the blood.

He came today, seven weeks after my accident, for my interview with Russ McQuillen, the investigator from the District Attorney's office for the state of Colorado. Mr. McQuillen took my statement to determine whether or not I had a case against the driver.

So, I had to tell him the story of the accident. I mean the whole story. Including the two beers and a cigarette.

When I related those particular details, my dad got up and left the room in disgust. I could see it on his face. Immediately I started dry heaving and vomiting. Anxiety, panic, dread -- a tidal wave of emotions flooded my system. He left; my father left me. I would have to face all this alone.

Then my mom rushed into the room. With that, my memory went blank. The interview ended.

Russ McQuillen was gone. And my father wasted no time telling me just how much I deserved everything that happened to me.

I had just sustained multiple pelvic fractures, including an infected pelvic hematoma. My right wrist fractured and had to be pinned back together. A fractured left foot, almost completely amputated in the crash, had to be sewn back on which also called for skin grafts. Severe lacerations on my legs and thighs, including a fourth-degree tear of my rectum and vagina which meant a colostomy to divert stool, as well as another skin graft. A horrific road burn covered my face from skidding across the road. Well, it could wait. The doctors and nurses worked on my body into the wee hours of the morning on that first night. None of them actually thought I would survive. Since then, my life has become a perpetual round of emergencies, surgery after surgery, and all with no end yet in sight.

And it's my fault. It's all my fault. The fact that I wasn't driving the car doesn't mean anything to my father in terms of my guilt. I made a bad decision and so I must suffer the consequences. That has always been his mantra to us.

Here's a religious math problem for you. Two beers, plus one cigarette, one nice-looking senior cadet, and a shiny convertible. Add them together and what do you get?

Obviously, the wrath of God.

Yes, the driver, Nate, had been drunk. In fact, tests done later revealed he had a blood alcohol level almost double the legal limit of .10 that night. But my father had told me not to drink or smoke, not Nate. And as the head of the household, my father is always right. He serves as God's representative here on earth, at least for our clan. Never once have I expressed my true feelings to him unless they were positive and aligned with family beliefs. Nor have I ever heard him say, "I'm sorry." Especially not now. I went against him—and therefore, against God. I had disappointed them both.

My father will never forgive me for this. I know it in my bones.

I guess I agree with him, too. I sinned. I deserve every bit of my horrific punishment from The Man Upstairs.

A New Heaven

I remember once asking my Lutheran pastor, why do bad things happen to good people?

I mean, I try so hard to do everything right. I've always thought I was a good girl. So why did this horrible car crash happen to me?

My pastor said that man has free will and God does not intervene in our decisions.

Hmmm. So how does that work exactly? Like in this case, I miraculously came back to life. Something must have intervened, even though I sinned. If that wasn't God, then I have no idea who else may have done it.

I find myself back in the confusion of Sunday School lessons in Hell. I can't make sense of it all.

Sitting in that hospital bed that day so many years ago, I only knew one thing for sure. I was going to have to work a whole lot harder at being a good girl. Then I might get my father, and therefore, God, to forgive me and make things right again. I had always pushed myself hard to please everyone else. But clearly not hard enough. I would have to put it into overdrive to make up for my huge mistake.

But on the other side of death, when I left my body, God had been all around me. God was in me. God was me, and I was God. God was presence and fullness and oneness. Most of all, God was love. Pure, no-strings-attached, open-arms love. In that state, I had not suddenly received forgiveness from a stern father for my mistakes. My "mistakes" just didn't exist. They never had. Nothing I had done on earth needed to be weighed or measured. The life I had just left behind told a story, yes, but just one of many I had lived in different realms.

Clearly the God of my childhood did not fit with what I had encountered out of my body. Looking back, I know this is a big reason why I didn't remember parts of my near-death experience until later in life. It did not fit with the belief system drilled into me by my parents—both before and after the wreck. As a result, I shoved down my memories of being there with God in pure bliss. (I'll share more later about how and why we suppress different experiences and aspects of ourselves.)

What I did remember from that experience, the white lights and the all-pervasive presence of love, I had no words for at the time. It looked nothing like what religion had taught me. I did not understand enough yet to call it God.

Your Beliefs About God Shape Your Relationship With Death

I now understand how much your beliefs about God shape your relationship with death. Here, I don't mean the beliefs you say you have. Things like "I am an atheist," or "I'm spiritual but not religious." These beliefs live in your intellect alone. I'm talking about the beliefs you truly hold, deep down, whether you want to or not.

Your real beliefs about God—most of them likely unconscious—were formed in early childhood. For most of us they came from the outside, usually from grownups, with lots of intensity attached.

Consider my story. I learned, again and again, to fear God. He would surely punish me. So, of course, I feared death.

Perhaps you grew up within a particular religious tradition like I did. Or maybe your parents never pushed you to believe anything. Still, their own attitudes about God had an influence of some kind on your own. Early experiences informed the beliefs you adopted or rejected, just as my own need to please my parents drove me to swallow everything they taught me.

Beliefs about God you took on, whether in childhood or later, directly impact your relationship with death.

If you're someone who doesn't have your own, clear understanding of God then death can scare you, because you don't really know what to expect when you die. What will happen to you?

If you don't believe in something greater than yourself, then you fear death because it will mean the end of you. (And, if you tell yourself that doesn't really scare you then I think you need to take a long, hard look at how honest you're being with yourself.)

Or maybe you, like so many of us, have more of a seven-layer dip of beliefs about God. On top you believe (intellectually) that God is love. Under that, you think God is watching for your mistakes and good deeds all the time in order to punish and reward you, a lot like Santa Claus. Then, deeper still, the God you made from your experiences holds the threat of wrath and vengeance. Or, maybe at the bottom of it all you believe in a God whose feelings you've somehow hurt with your misdeeds. You spend your life trying to make up for it.

In any of these examples you definitely don't feel excited about what waits for you at the end of your life.

To create a healthy relationship with death, you must create a healthy relationship with God. Not just on the surface, but in what you deeply believe. You must become aware of what you've hidden from yourself, bring it to the surface, and find ways to heal the wounds that shaped your ideas about God.

Where is God?

Here I am, yet again, lying in my bed. I am fifty years old now, and the car accident, decades behind me. But I'm still hurting from it. In fact, I am in so much pain I had to take medical leave from my job as the Wellness Director of Adventist Health Castle and start an experimental medication that included methadone.

God, how much of my life have I spent lying in bed? My head throbbing with pain, fatigued, dealing with yet another immune challenge, and feeling depressed. I ask myself, where is God in all this suffering and pain?

In fact, where is God, period? I believe in Him, and know He is there somewhere. I talk to my angels and guides daily. Pray. Meditate. I stay open to signs and look deeper into their meanings when they reveal themselves. Isn't this enough?

Today, though, I realize it isn't. I'm missing something. But what?

I'm not sure how to participate in a relationship with an entity I cannot see, feel, hear, touch, etc. I pray to the benevolent being I say I believe in, yes. So where is my confirmation from Him? I want proof. Demonstration from God that He heard me. Or even just a clear sense of what action steps I need to take next.

But all I feel is more pain.

To feel this bad for this long... regular migraines for three decades now. Well, God is just not coming through for me.

I reach for another Imitrex pill, the migraine medication I have been on for at least 20 years. This is my fourth one this week; I've reached my limit.

And I'm tired of trying.

Later...

Somehow, I mustered the strength to walk seventy yards to "our" beautiful Kailua beach.

"God, what does a relationship with you look like? Help me here."

Soft sand squishes under my toes. The brilliant turquoise of Pacific Ocean waves curl, then fold against the shore.

It strikes me: God is alive in nature. The ocean. The sand. Everything that has energy, actually. God is this eternal, overarching, positive, energy. It spans billions of galaxies, and even beyond time and space. And at the same time, God continuously focuses unconditional love and light on me.

In this moment, the belief that the only way to have a personal relationship with God is to be "saved in Jesus Christ" suddenly seems so childish. Sorry, Baptist faith, but it does. Because I'm having a real "come to Jesus" moment right now. I get, not intellectually but in my bones, that I am an expression of God, one of the rays of God beaming out from the heart of creation. You know, all those white lights. They are me. They are you. Each of us carries the essence of God within us.

The power is not out there somewhere. It is in each one of us.

A New Relationship to God

This moment of time would completely change my life. I was waking up to my own sovereignty.

I already believed in sovereignty, intellectually speaking. I would have described it this way. I am the one creating my life. I am making the choices, sometimes consciously and sometimes unconsciously. My personality might see and understand my choices at some points, and at others, my Higher Self or my soul may have made a choice. I'm no victim in all this, especially not God's victim.

I was waking up to all of this in my felt experience. Inside I was thinking and feeling along these lines: I'm God's dance partner. More than that, too. I am God. I am a God-me, having a turn around the ballroom with life itself. Nothing outside me, no person, place, or thing has the power to complete me. Only this God-me. The life force is pumping itself through my veins, and through all of the world around me.

When I say all this, I don't mean I was egotistically equating myself with the all-powerful "Godman" I had learned about in Sunday School. To say, "I am God," did not mean I saw myself as omniscient or without mistakes. Instead, I was realizing those ideas of God were wrong all along. God is the spark of light that keeps my heart beating. The more I fan its flame, the more I embody myself as God.

That day on the beach, the revelation of it felt sudden and even startling. Looking back, though, I see that I had been traveling toward it most of my life.

As a child, my prayer requests generally were answered in my favor. Truly bad things rarely befell me. My grandfather died when I was five, yes; but he was an alcoholic, ate poorly, and smoked cigars, so no one seemed surprised when he had a heart attack at age fifty-eight. Besides, I barely knew him. It didn't really touch me. Later, my sister was thrown from a horse in a terrible accident in Yosemite National Park. Then she recovered. Other things, like being whipped by my father with a belt, I felt I deserved. I didn't bother praying for him to stop. I also didn't waste my time praying for trivial things, like making cheerleader. When I didn't, I knew that was on me, not The Man Upstairs. All my rote prayers about everything else seemed to be getting God's stamp of approval. What did I know back then about "Thy will be done?"

When I was processed into the AFA, the nature of my prayers took on a more urgent tone. I had no family around to protect me from the onslaught of slings and arrows I daily endured.

Please help me survive the Obstacle, Assault, and Confidence courses I would beg. Please help me not to fail again. Oh, Lord, please just help me not to fall over and die. I cannot do another push-up, God. I cannot run another mile; I will surely collapse.

But all of those prayers seemed to be going into some piled-up inbox on God's desk that He seemed too busy to review. I survived Hell Week purely by some miracle. Things never got easier for me. I always lagged behind the others on the courses; my grades registered at the bottom of the class. My senior year in high school, I thoroughly enjoyed my service on a fashion board putting together runway shows for charity. Now I was enduring simulations of life in a P.O.W. camp and S.E.R.E (Survival, Escape, Resistance, and Evasion) in the Rocky Mountains. Instead of how to grammatically parse a sentence, I was getting schooled in how to kill. I could not muster even a shred of interest, much less enthusiasm, for any of it. Fear, panic, anxiety, dread—in short, a sense of impending doom shadowed me day and night. I just stuffed it down. I had to give all my energy to reacting to the next command someone barked at me.

When allowed (usually Sunday early mornings), I would go to the Cadet Chapel. I marveled at the beauty of it, truly an architectural wonder. But I felt no connection to the God of this place, whoever He was. Wasn't He supposed to help me, love me, bring me comfort? I went through the motions, hoping all that stuff I grew up believing would prove true. But I felt nothing.

Perhaps it won't surprise you to learn that as early as boot camp I began to question God. I was surviving the AFA through willpower alone. I knew I could not keep this up for four years - heck the first year nearly killed me. Where was that God from the Bible drills, the one who was supposed to be, "an ever-present help in times of trouble"? I could find no evidence of his succor. Rather, my reward for all the earnest seeking came in the form of yet more scouring by the AFA. Of course, my dignity had gotten scrubbed away long ago. By my sophomore year (called a third degree), though, I was starting to feel like I was losing my sanity. God, you're just not coming through for me, here.

As I questioned God, I also began to stray from the rules my father had drilled into me. At first, I only flirted with the idea of disobeying him. Gradually my proverbial toe of doubt became a foot of disbelief. And so on. Like so many others before me, I was groping toward my own understanding of the world. Fumbling towards sovereignty, you might say. Pretty soon I had gone so far as to drink two beers and smoke a cigarette.

Dang it. Why did my father have to be right?

At least that's how I felt in that hospital bed. If only I had listened to him. But no, I had to go and sin. Clearly God was punishing me. At least on some level, I agreed with my father that I deserved what I got.

I had to agree with him. For many months after the accident, I had to rely on him and my mother just to get through each day, as I had in childhood. The pursuit of sovereignty took a back seat to my body's survival.

Things didn't end there, though. Once my body had recovered enough for me to function more independently, I continued to struggle with the God of my childhood.

Long after I left the hospital, doubts in the religion of my parents persisted—and grew. I kept trading in my churches. I would leave this one, which couldn't give me any satisfying answers, for a newer, more open-minded one. Eventually I found myself attending one that proclaimed the power of positive thinking as its central doctrine. I embraced its tenets wholeheartedly, too. I could recite positive affirmations like self-help guru Louise Hay had taught me and found more comfort here than I had in the Cadet Chapel. Over time, I became well versed in the philosophy of sovereignty that this church, and the many books I read, all preached.

Lasting change does not happen overnight for any of us, though. I've come to distrust anyone who touts the five easy steps to X, Y, or Z. Transformation takes work. Focus. Dedication. Reading about sovereignty or hearing about it on Sunday morning all helped but living as a sovereign being requires so much more.

I had experienced the true power of the Oneness I now understand God to be when I left my body at death. I would re-experience it again later, when the fullness of the near-death experience resurfaced. But my body and personality needed time and support to catch up with those experiences. All these years had passed on the outside. Inside, however, I was still lying in that hospital bed, immobilized—not just from injuries but by my father's vicious self-righteousness.

My Vending Machine God

That's exactly how an unconscious belief works. Maybe at first you make it up in response to something that happens to you. "It's my fault my mother died," or "I could have stopped my parents' divorce if I had been a better kid." Or maybe someone else tells you to believe it, as in "You brought this on yourself, Nicole." Then the belief gets repeated, over and over again, sometimes outside of you, like at church or by a parent. But at some point, you take on the belief yourself. You keep repeating it inside yourself, even if it harms you. In time, you don't even realize you're doing it anymore. The body keeps that belief active in your system, whether you want it there or not.

Even though you use your mind and thoughts to create a belief like this, ultimately it isn't about thinking. Rather, it becomes woven into your emotions and physiology. What I call "root beliefs" become so anchored in your system that you may have a hard time even seeing that you carry them. They create a vibrational resonance that shapes how you look at the world, how you interpret your experiences, even the people and experiences you draw into your life.

In my case, I have been functioning for most of my life with a root belief in a Vending Machine God. Put your good deeds into the vending machine, just like money, and voila! Out come your rewards. Right?

My identity as a people pleaser—and in this case, a GOD-pleaser—lies at the heart of the matter. If I could just work hard enough to make God happy, I would finally make everything come out differently. The migraines would stop. I would miraculously return to rosy-cheeked health. God would give me my rewards.

Now I see it, though. God is not like Santa Claus, making a list and checking it twice. He is not a benevolent genie looking down from the sky, waiting to grant my wishes. God is impersonal, meaning not an object or person in any sense I can conceive of with my limited mind. God is everywhere. God is love, but not in a form that the human mind can grasp. Constant, and constantly moving, a life force that is not born and does not die.

Paradoxically, God is also me. The truest, most real part of me.

To be honest, the whole thing kind of freaks me out. This understanding of God is moving out of my intellect and into my nervous system. It's shaking me, to my very cells.

At the same time, I feel so alive. Empowered. I am a creator, drawing on the great intelligence of life within me. I am God, taking on a physical form.

That word "fear," which I've been taught from church to associate with God, can function as a noun or a verb. As the latter, you can use it as in being afraid of someone or something that is likely to be dangerous, painful, or threatening. Yup. That's how I always saw God. Even if I expected goodies, I also knew at some point the other shoe would drop. God's shoe, I mean. Right on me.

There's another way to use that word, though, straight out of the King James Bible. There, the word "fear" often means, "awe and reverence." In all the NDEs I've read about, I haven't encountered stories of shame or fear, but rather, sacred encounters that point to our connections.

Somehow this moment on the beach feels like a death blow—pun intended—for my worn out, vending machine version of God.

Who is God?

In a way, I have written this whole book to answer that one question. It's the one my life has revolved around, even before the accident, but especially afterwards.

But I admit, I can't actually answer the question. Not in this book, or any other. At least not with a pat phrase or two. Words just won't cut it.

You must experience God to know God.

The part-time work I do today is working with clients (including children) to reduce mind and body stress. I think of a six-year-old client of mine. When I asked her how she sees God, she eagerly told me, "God is a blue spirit with colors and balloons in all different colors, no head and can talk." Clearly this little girl is still having a direct experience with God, no filters from other people involved. Her understanding inspired me and her parents.

Your own experience of God will probably look nothing like hers or mine. Yet, I hope my story gives you the encouragement to continue on that path. Whether you've just begun or spent a lifetime already in the pursuit, you will surely never reach the end of the road.

CHAPTER 5: BABY STEPS

Lesson 5:
*Loving ourselves and others is the most important thing we can do.**

Homecoming

Please, don't touch me. Please, don't touch me.

I've arrived home in Jackson, Mississippi. When we left the hospital in Colorado, a fresh coating of snow covered the ground. Here, only the Christmas muzak signals the season. My friends and family came to the airport to greet me. They filled the gateway with flowers, shouts of joy, homemade banners that spelled out, "WELCOME HOME!" But from my wheelchair, already doubled over in pain, I could only find one thought.

Please, don't touch me.

Even the slightest touch sent sharp pains through my abdomen. Actually, even breathing hurt.

I had just spent four months in the hospital—two hospitals, to be precise. I've mentioned the fractures in my pelvis, wrist, and foot, the lacerations, skin grafts, colostomy. They took out my gallbladder, too. I survived multiple infections, including sepsis and gangrene in my right leg. At one point my lungs filled with fluid, and I came close to drowning in my own bed. In all, I've lived through six major operations in the last third of a year, two of them featuring a Code Blue, meaning, both my heart and breathing had stopped. Along the way, I have received a whopping sixty-four pints of blood. Oh, and I became addicted to morphine, Demerol, and Valium after seven weeks of continuous use every four hours. The withdrawal from them nearly killed me all over again because my dad ordered it to be cold turkey.

---

* Source: https://mcusercontent.com/6aeb61681f6c311e999fff730/files/5070a118-63b3-4ac3-87f4-08b4f5d6e2e0/2020_IANDS_Annual_Report.01.pdf pg. 15

I know I should feel grateful. I am home. And the hospital lies behind me. I can finally get on with creating a life for myself. But after being away from home and coming back as basically an infant it was a huge set-back for me emotionally and spiritually. Mom was focused on feeding me since I had lost so much weight and driving me to all my appointments. Making me as comfortable as possible. Dad was absorbed once again in his work and occasionally we would play Monopoly or watch TV together - and of course always church. My siblings were off in college and my younger brother was at the MMA. The "worst" seemed to have passed but I felt lonely and disconnected. Everyone was going on with their lives and I felt left behind. My mom became my best friend - not healthy in my case. Every little success - being able to go to the bathroom on my own - was a huge milestone that only we two celebrated. So for eight months we bonded even closer at 6152 Waverly Dr. in Jackson! I had my mother's rapt attention for a full year. Hence, the devastation for me when she was "taken" away from me by my dad.

I had my life, and this new "friendship" with my mom, but what is my life supposed to look like exactly? Especially now that I am home with my parents and emotionally, physically, and mentally bruised, broken, scarred, and hurting. I'm more than relieved I won't be going back to the Air Force Academy. But where would I go? Never before had I considered what I wanted to do or be.

I didn't need to think about it too hard. My father had a clear idea of what he wanted from me next. Besides, I couldn't think about it. Literally could not. Too. Much. Pain.

The Spectre of... Life

My spirit flew out of my body before it hit the ground. On the other side of death, I experienced the exact opposite of pain. Pure bliss.

I can assure you, firsthand, that the moment of death comes without any pain attached. To this day, I do not remember even a moment of discomfort during death. Rather, it was a simple, instantaneous transition to a truly wonderful place. We do indeed have much awaiting us to look forward to at death.

Still, most people I know walk through life in "death denial." They pretend it won't happen to them and act surprised when it befalls someone they know, scarcely able to admit, even to themselves, the litany of questions about it that follow them around: When? How? Will it hurt? Will that really be the end?

I don't blame them, of course. I certainly wasn't thinking of death at age nineteen. Back then, I more or less thought of myself as immortal, even if I never admitted that to myself in so many words. I grew up in a culture that did not educate or socialize me to understand death or dying. In my world, death finally came along after you'd done your time in a nursing home – you know, those sad places full of bad smells and blue-haired ladies calling out for your attention. Of course, the fire-and-brimstone preachers at the church talked about death plenty of times. But they weren't actually trying to help me prepare for the inevitability of death. Rather, they were using fear to control my actions.

Not every culture ignores death, though. I heard an Asian, Indian spiritual master explain her own upbringing around the topic. As a child, maybe four or five years old, her parents took her to a funeral. They encouraged her to touch the body. The dead man felt cold, they explained, because his spirit was gone. He would never return again to visit them. Beyond this funeral experience, the topic of death came up daily in their house. As her father left their home each day, he would make a point of kissing all of his children, even if they had not yet risen from bed. "We don't know if this is the last time we will see one another," he would say every time. "The God of death could come for me today, or for you."

Though my family never talked about death, I was indoctrinated into strong beliefs about it. As a good person who believed in God, I would die and go to heaven. Heaven had streets of gold, I was told, and pearly gates. I had nothing else to go on beyond that. No one, not even the pastor, could tell me precisely when I would die. And none of the things I learned in church about God, heaven, angels, or the devil and hell, for that matter, prepared me for the actual experience I had on the other side.

In a book I read called *Intimate Death*, author Marie de Hennezel relates the story of a little boy dying of cancer. She shared his message. "I know I am only here for a limited period of time, to learn something. When I learn what I've been born to learn, I'll leave. But in my head, I cannot imagine life stopping." The unknowable aspects of death, the sheer unfathomable nature of it, can leave anyone, from any culture, feeling uncomfortable.

Still, I do think that the Indian girl's parents did her a great service when they taught her to recognize the presence of death in her daily life. Surely the practice engendered in her a greater appreciation for life. She understood the importance of making her time here count.

Which brings me to what I believe is the biggest reason most people fear death: They don't know how to live.

I certainly didn't. I had gotten myself so twisted up in pleasing other people that I could not imagine, much less describe, true joy. I couldn't have given a name to the experience of fulfillment if it had walked up to me on the street and introduced itself. No dictionary, no matter how precise, could have offered me insight into the meanings of words like these since I had so little experience with them.

I know I'm not alone, either. Only on their deathbeds do most people finally surrender to the call of life to turn inward, toward meaning and purpose. Consider the billions—yes, billions!—of dollars we Americans spend every year on improving our looks. According to the U. S. Food and Drug Administration Americans spent an estimated $30 billion in 1992 on all types of diet programs and products, including diet foods and drinks. Add to that anti-aging creams, gym memberships, and plastic surgeries, just to name a few. It boggles the mind.

If we spent even a fraction of this on self-realization, how much fuller would our lives be? And how much more prepared for death we would find ourselves. To face death fearlessly, you have to have connected deeply with yourself during your life.

I'm not saying this comes easily. Knowing you want to live fully, and doing it, can be miles apart. Why?

Some of the reasons I've already mentioned. Our identities drive us, along with our unconscious limiting beliefs. Memories that we suppress play a role, along with the lingering effects of painful experiences we do recall, especially those with powerful emotions attached. It makes for quite a list, once tallied.

In a way, we are haunted, not by death, but by living. As American poet Mary Oliver asks, "What will you do with your one wild and precious life?"

Rehab 1983-1984

"Holy @#%&!"

Did I say that out loud? Shoot. As a good Christian woman, I know I should not be uttering such choice phrases. During the crash the peroneal nerve on my right leg was severed. Of all the injuries—the sprains, the broken bones, dislocations, lacerations—nerve damage comes with the most pain by far. Sometimes the pain from it is so bad that I'm sure even Jesus would utter a few @#%&!s.

To be fair, the pain had improved since I returned to Mississippi. I started rehab in Colorado. It had been brutal. In Mississippi they used transcutaneous electrical nerve stimulation (TENS) to help control the pain. It helped, for sure. Still, I could hardly call rehab a pleasure cruise. Pain still dominated the process.

The rehab pain took a different shape than the pain I had endured at the airport and upon arriving home. The day after we got back, Mom took me to the doctor. Again. (As if the two of us hadn't already spent enough time with doctors.) Turns out I had a kidney infection. Mom had worried it was pneumonia, so the diagnosis brought her some relief. All I could think was, well, here we go again.

Then the holidays came. Our house looked a lot like Grand Central Station for a while. Tons of people dropped by to say hello and hear about the accident, and Mom worried the whole time that I would pick up dangerous germs. But I liked having so many people around to distract me.

Then came the new year, and with it, new rehab. For me it seemed more like years, though. Three times a week, Mississippi Baptist Hospital and I had a standing date.

Therapists started me in a wheelchair and water therapy. Recovering from a broken pelvis, ankle, and wrist made it feel less like therapy, though, and more like medieval torture at first. Trying to achieve something akin to a simple free stroke or breaststroke exhausted me, no kidding. In the beginning, one lap wore me out. My cheerleader, Mom, kept reminding me that water therapy provided the "most painless" way for me to rebuild my strength. Trust me, though. There was nothing painless about it.

Eventually I did get stronger. I graduated to crutches specially designed for someone with a broken wrist and foot. I begin to get the hang of them, too. I had a lovely cane to look forward to after the crutches. Baby steps, baby steps they kept telling me.

I would walk again. I was determined.

The hardest part of rehab, though? It's loneliness. Since Christmas, I had not seen much of my old friends. Even if they came over, what could we talk about? Military drills? The pleasures of medication withdrawal? Maybe we'd gossip on the joys of knowing I wouldn't get asked out any time soon. (Ever?) Or I guess I could have told them all about the fun of being dependent on your mom to go to the bathroom.

At least rehab gave me some more independence. Sort of. Even if I didn't have to rely on my parents anymore for every single step I took, I still carried around the weight of knowing how deeply I'd disappointed them. Every single day, I faced it. When I picked up my crutches. When I lived through yet another day with no social life. When I looked in the mirror and saw my new, scarred-up face, the one I still can't actually believe is mine now. My father told my brothers and sister, "Look at Nicole. That's what happens when you disobey me."

The excruciating pain of rehab didn't even touch the pain of hearing this. If anything could hurt worse, I don't know what it could have been.

Understanding Trauma

After I endured four months of hospital time after the crash, I faced eight months of intensive rehab. Learning to walk again stretched my patience to the limits. My full rehabilitation didn't end there, either. I would spend years in physical recovery. To this day, in fact, my right foot has not fully healed from the nerve damage. My toes remain more or less paralyzed; I have no control over or feeling them. Any footwear I buy requires a strap in the back, so no slides or slippers for me. This lingering issue may seem relatively small, but it caused some challenges while living in the Hawaiian Islands later in my life. It's one of those details that most people take for granted. (Please don't.)

This serves as one example of physical trauma. Medicine often uses the word "trauma" to refer to serious bodily injury. In the crash, my body had sustained multiple traumatic injuries.

Most of the time, physical trauma like this leads to emotional trauma as well. In fact, the American Psychological Association defines trauma as, "an emotional response to a terrible event like an accident, rape, or natural disaster." In the next two chapters, I'll go much deeper into the mechanics of trauma in the brain. Here, I'll share that symptoms of emotional trauma can include anxiety, unresponsiveness, night terrors, edginess, poor concentration, mood swings – and often some combination of any of these. This kind of response to an overwhelmingly negative event, while completely normal, if left untreated often leaves a person unable to lead a normal life.

In my story, both in this chapter and in others, you'll find many vestiges of emotional trauma. Of course, as stated above, you do not have to endure physical trauma like I did to experience emotional trauma. Other things/events can also spark emotional trauma. Small children are especially vulnerable to it.

By now, most of us know something about emotional trauma thanks to the work of pioneering psychiatrists like Bessel van der Kolk, M.D. Less frequently, though, people realize that emotional trauma can impact the physical body.

To understand this a little better, consider the way that neuropeptides function. Neuropeptides are biological messengers released by the brain, sent throughout the body, and accepted by receptor sites located on the cells of every tissue, organ, and body part you have. We have known for a long time about neuropeptides, such as endorphins (our happy hormones), serotonin (the feel-good chemical), vasopressin (the blood pressure regulator), and insulin (controller of metabolism and sugar).

Now let's turn to the work of an internationally recognized neuroscientist and pharmacologist, Dr. Candace Pert. In her lifetime, she published more than 250 research articles. Along the way she discovered emotional molecules, a type of neuropeptide which can change the chemistry and electricity of every cell in the body. In other words, she found under the microscope that your emotions are actually physical chemicals that can help or hurt you. Your body constantly registers, in a tangible way, every word that you say—as well as every thought you think.

Ever heard the phrase, "I can't stomach that person/situation"? What about, "I have a lump in my throat." From experience, you know you're not making it up. The sensation exists in your body. Emotional messenger molecules are landing on the receptor sites to create a physical response. Dr. Pert's work demonstrates how your state of mind changes your body and your health.

The Family Legacy of Trauma

Every person deals with trauma differently. Some can witness horrors without suffering the side effect of emotional trauma. Others find themselves extremely susceptible to it. Researchers don't fully understand why. But they can point to risk factors. A previous traumatic experience that is not healed can make you much more likely to experience trauma again.

Some also think your family history can play a role in your trauma response.

Consider a 2013 study in Nature Neuroscience. Researchers blew the scent of cherry blossoms into the cages of male mice while zapping their feet with electric shocks. Before long, the mice associated this smell with pain—a classic Pavlovian response. One whiff of cherry blossoms made the mice agitated and jumpy.

Then the researchers bred these male mice. To be sure that the offspring mice would not learn their fathers' jumpy behavior through example, researchers separated the pups from their genetic parents. Instead, mice who had not received the smell-shock treatments raised the test subject pups. Still, the pups became far more nervous and jumpier at the smell of cherry blossoms than the pups of fathers who had not received the smell-shock treatments. Then, their pups, the grandchildren of the mice who had received the shock-smell treatments, also showed sensitivity to the scent of cherry blossoms. Neither of the subsequent generations showed sensitivity to any other smells besides this one.

The study author, Dr. Brian Dias, of Emory's Yerkes National Primate Research Center and other scientists attribute these results to epigenetics, the study of the changes that happen to us through the modification of how we express our genes. The DNA you carry does not change. How that DNA is expressed, however, certainly can. And it seems likely you can inherit certain epigenetic tendencies from your family.

This study has helped me gain a much wider context for my own response to trauma. When you hear the life stories of my parents, you'll probably understand why.

In 1941, at the tender age of three, my Ukrainian mother and her family fled Russia when Germany invaded their country. Her father was arrested in Kiev by Soviet authorities, never to be heard from again - hence executed. They relocated to Germany. There she witnessed her grandmother's death, along with the loss of her home again, this time by Allied bombs. Then she endured seven years in a Displaced Persons' Camp, first under Nazi rule and then in postwar Germany. To survive, her mother married a widower, and the family emigrated to America in 1951. At thirteen, my mother found herself in Holly Springs, Mississippi, living not the American dream, but as an indentured servant of the church who had sponsored her own family's move to the States. Her teenage years were spent not at sock hops but out in the fields, picking cotton. On top of the violence in the larger world, my mom lived daily with the brutality of her own parents, who struggled to cope with the turbulence and horror they had survived.

In all of this, my mom found refuge in only one place: The God of the Lutheran Church.

My father also lived through his own nightmares. His father drank far too much alcohol. Many times, my father would find himself at the local jail, bailing out his dad. Not a pretty scene. Also, not the worst thing his father did. I will never forget my father telling me about the time his dad took my father's dog out in the back yard and shot him. Dead. (To be clear, this was not an act of compassion for a dying animal with mange.) To this day, my father has told me very little about his childhood, a fairly common phenomenon for a man of his generation who has grown up with violence and needing to keep up a certain societal image. But I think this one story speaks volumes about what he must have lived with on a daily basis. His mom was an immigrant from Ireland with a 3rd grade education who came to America for a better life. She suffered from mental disease and in the early 1970's underwent the standard treatment at that time, electric shock therapy. She lived the last twenty years of her life in a nursing home across the street from her own home.

In the end, my father came to the same conclusions as my mother. Only God could help him—which is to say, the God of his local Southern Baptist church. God, and the military, that is. One gave him solace, the other, a way out.

If researchers who studied mice and the smell of cherry blossoms got it right, then imagine the epigenetic legacy of trauma I have inherited. I have two parents who had faced serious adversities before they reached the age of twenty.

It goes beyond epigenetics, though. My parents did not simply pass along a genetic tendency to express my DNA in a certain way. They also taught me their own ways of handling trauma.

Research has shown that to heal trauma, it has to be directly addressed. This can take many different forms. The one thing that definitely does not work. Ignoring it.

Yet this was the main strategy my parents passed on to me.

Just after the accident, my mother turned more than ever to her faith in God. And I do believe her faith helped carry all of us through the worst parts of this crisis, myself and my father included. I'm sure her experiences as a child and young woman, as well as how she had learned to deal with these experiences, had prepared her to do this well.

Still, Mom had no tools, training, or experience in how to recover from the crisis once the emergency had passed. Apart from sharing some of the surface details of their childhood experiences, I doubt she or my father ever did anything to meaningfully address the pain of their histories. Certainly, I never saw them express the feelings those experiences had caused. Instead, they had both learned to bottle them up. They relied on highly rigid thought and social systems to help keep all those bottled emotions in check.

So, after the accident, I got clear advice. Buck up. Pray hard. Jesus is your therapist, after all. Follow his will and blame yourself for your mistakes in the hopes that you can avoid them in the future. Keep all your coping strategies (like people pleasing) firmly, unwaveringly in place. Most of all, do not talk about your real feelings—if you even know what they are. Probably you don't.

Maybe it sounds cruel to send your daughter messages like these. Indeed, it felt cruel to me. But now more than ever, I understand. My parents gave me the best support they could, given their own limitations. In their generation, psychologists were for "crazy people," not themselves. To be fair to them, psychology has only begun to find effective methods for healing trauma, especially PTSD, in the last few decades.

Spiritual Trauma

Along with physical and emotional trauma, I would like to introduce the notion of spiritual trauma.

Let's be clear. Your spirit cannot be traumatized. It is whole, perfect, and complete. Never can you or another person harm or destroy it. As Spirit, you are eternal.

When I refer to spiritual trauma, I am not talking about trauma that happens to your Spirit. Rather, I'm pointing to the trauma you experience as a result of the misguided belief that you are separate from God. This belief causes fallout for your whole body-mind-emotional system.

Of course, my story illustrates this phenomenon overtly. I grew up inside of a religion that actively promoted a God outside of me. The God of this tradition judges, punishes, and even condemns people to eternal suffering. All of that left me feeling deeply afraid of God. In my life, I found ways to punish myself, just like I believed God would do; I would beat God to the punch, or else project that God had done it to me. Unconsciously, I believed that God wanted me to struggle, strain, and live a small life of lack. So, I did.

This God looks nothing like the God I had experienced on the other side of the veil. That God, a force of love, light, joy, peace, bliss, and complete fullness, would never have me live inside this cramped, mean, and tiny world that arose from the God of my childhood. This God has also given all of us complete free will. So, I was free to create all those limitations for myself if I wanted.

But you don't have to grow up in a religion to suffer from spiritual trauma. Nearly all of us deal with it, in fact. In Western countries we have inherited the notion of original sin. The Christian doctrine of original sin tells us that we are born bad. We can do nothing to make the situation better. Even if you were not raised Christian, you have lived your life steeped in the legacy of this doctrine. It has woven its way into nearly every aspect of how Western cultures view the world, even if not overtly stated.

Don't believe me? Well, I'll bet you've overheard yourself saying something to yourself like, "I'm not good enough." If you have the creative force of God inside you, how could that ever be true? The effort to prove ourselves, that we all seem to deal with, arises at least in part from the unconscious cultural belief that God disapproves of us. We believe God wants us to live in shame.

I love an anecdote about the Dalai Lama on this topic. When someone explained to him the notion of original sin, he took three whole days to digest the information. At the end of that time, he said that he now understood so many things about Western culture that previously had baffled him.

In his own culture, children learn that they are expressions of God, born whole. Over time, human ignorance covers over that perfect spark of the divine, until it is forgotten. The purpose of spiritual practice, then, is to reconnect with the God-spark, and fan that spark, until it becomes a blazing fire which consumes all human forgetfulness and ignorance.

Even in that culture and others like it, however, I suspect spiritual trauma exists. I've already shared about the gap between intellectual beliefs and integrated understanding. Someone truly free of a belief in their separation from God will no longer experience fear or lack. Instead, she rests in the knowledge that she is everywhere, in everything, with access to anything she needs at any time.

If you don't believe this is possible, I encourage you to explore the lives of people like the Dalai Lama and others who have dedicated themselves to healing the human legacy of spiritual trauma.

Soul Parts Reunited

"I have to admit, I have never seen anything like this, so I need to ask my guides what it is."

Shaman Scott has just paused. The year is 2019, and I have come to him for a soul retrieval. On my own, I probably would not have sought out someone like a Shaman for this kind of healing work. In fact, it's taken me three years to follow up on my friend's suggestion to reach out to him. But I have known for a while that I need a fresh approach to my healing, so I decided to take the leap.

"Nicole, I'm looking at your energy body," the Shaman continues. "It has a huge crack coming from the top, almost like a lightning bolt. Your Spirit and life force, your Soul, was leaving through this crack when you had your near-death experience. That's because at death, the energy body cracks all the way open, from the top down, and the Soul is set free. Nicole, your energy cracked about 30% from the top down during the accident. And it's still cracked."

I felt stunned. Shaman Scott's words sounded faraway. Was I reliving some part of the original experience of leaving my body? Something more than words was washing over me as he spoke.

"At the time of the crash, you made a soul agreement that has kept you stuck in terror and shock. You decided, 'It is not safe to let go and have fun because disaster can strike at any minute.'

"Also, I see that an entity of judgment still lurks above your crown. Looks like it comes from your parents. Did they blame you for the accident? It looks like they blamed you instead of supporting you with compassion and love."

His insights astonish me. How could he understand all this just by looking at my energy field? I have mentioned the accident, yes, but I gave him no details about my family and not much about my current life, either.

Throughout the session, I have been feeling a presence (more than one?) of loving compassion all around me. As he works, Shaman Scott periodically says something like "This is now healed," or "Now it is done." With this, a rush of movement spreads through me, not in my body, exactly, but more like in parts of me I can sense but not see.

Near the end of the session, Shaman Scott describes something he is witnessing. Streams and streams of soul parts are coming back home to me from the hundreds of times I've gone into fight or flight since the accident. Then comes the first part of me that left, the one that went out at the time of the accident. As he speaks of it, a wave of relief washes over me.

"This part of you was ready to go into the White Light and leave this plane. But now your energy body has been repaired. This part of you now knows it's safe to stay here, in your body."

A new agreement now replaces the old one, he tells me. Instead of living from the dread that God could punish me at any moment, I am free to fulfill my life purpose.

From Fragmentation to Wholeness

In the weeks and months after this soul retrieval, I did indeed enjoy a new sense of freedom and purpose. In fact, I finally started working in earnest on this book, a project I have felt called to for decades. But I never could quite get it off the ground – until now.

I've shared my experience of this session because I believe it illustrates beautifully the process of healing from any kind of trauma. By this I do not mean that we all need to see a shamanic healer for a soul retrieval. But I do think that trauma in any form leaves us feeling fragmented.

In reality, you are whole, perfect, and complete. Though I said this earlier, it bears repeating. Through the lens of trauma, however, you experience yourself in disjointed pieces. It's like visiting the funhouse mirrors at a carnival or looking at a reflection of yourself in broken glass.

The effort it takes to live from a fragmented version of yourself uses up a lot of energy. Imagine trying to get dressed every day in front of one of those funhouse mirrors. You would add irritation, frustration, confusion, and a host of other emotions to the simple process of getting ready for work. Exhausting.

I'll offer another way to understand how trauma steals away your life force, based in neuroscience. The parts of your brain where trauma gets lodged, the amygdalae and corresponding structures, do not function with past tense. Until a traumatic experience is resolved, it has not ended. Instead, the brain functions like the event is still happening, right now.

Consider what that means. Were you horribly shamed by a teacher at age eight? Well, you are still being shamed by that teacher every single day until you release the trauma from the areas of your brain where it lives – whether or not you realize it. You can see the evidence of it, though. Maybe you suddenly explode at your wife when she asks you about a minor mistake you made with your checkbook last month. In that moment, she is not your wife, but rather, that unkind teacher.

When you heal trauma, you suddenly have more energy freed up for the good stuff in life – stuff like authoring a book, for instance.

My intention is not to give you a prescription for exactly how to heal trauma. So many different methods work well – EMDR, brain spotting, body-centered psychotherapy, Neuro Emotional Technique (NET), just to name a few. More than anything, I hope to inspire you to pursue something. It may take trial and error, but you can find something that will work for you.

Acing this Mandatory Curriculum

All of us have endured trauma. And for all of us, those experiences leave traces. Physical trauma can lead to emotional scarring. Emotional trauma can cause physical conditions. And spiritual trauma, that nagging sense that we have irredeemably separated ourselves from God, weaves its way through all of it.

Making peace with death means making peace with life. Trauma, and the suffering we create around it, can keep us locked in the past. Over and over, we relive something that is no longer happening, even though the brain makes us think it is. Life becomes a battlefield.

But healing the past creates the space to follow your heart. You can enjoy, more and more, the pleasure of being in a body.

And if you live fully, you can die fully. When your time to cross the threshold comes, you can say, "I have used my time well. Now I am ready to go."

CHAPTER 6: FORGETTING

Lesson 6: *We are more than our physical body and brain.**

Night Sweats

From a deep sleep I bolted awake. My heartbeat raced; the thin, pale-purple cotton nightgown I wore was soaked in sweat. Am I safe? I looked around, trying to figure out if I was still in danger. Was someone after me or was it just a dream?

I glanced at the digital clock. 12:30 a.m. I had only slept an hour and a half. Clearly the anti-anxiety drug I took earlier in the evening wasn't working. The night sweats, coming from my chest, right between my breasts, were getting worse.

I got up and changed my nightshirt, grabbed a cool washcloth and wiped my chest down. Then I headed for my usual haunt, the kitchen. Food calmed me down. It always does.

I opened the freezer and grabbed a pint of Ben and Jerry's coffee frozen yogurt (fewer calories than ice cream). Grabbing a spoon, I headed upstairs to the safety of my bedroom. Into my king-size bed I crawled, clutching my stuffed animal, Boo, as I mechanically started eating the yogurt. Its coolness soothed the heat of my body.

Once I had polished off the entire pint, I curled into the fetal position. Who cared about brushing teeth? I was finally falling back to sleep, which matters a whole lot more than clean teeth.

Two hours later, I woke again, still anxious. Back down to the kitchen. This time I stuck a bag of Orville Redenbacher into the microwave.

---

* Source: https://mcusercontent.com/6aeb61681f6c311e999fff730/files/5070a118-63b3-4ac3-87f4-08b4f5d6e2e0/2020_IANDS_Annual_Report.01.pdf pg. 15

That would do it. As I waited for the bag to finish popping, I polished off a couple of slices of extra sharp cheddar cheese.

Numbly, I climbed up the twelve steps to my big, safe bedroom. In bed again, I shoved fistfuls of buttered popcorn into my mouth with the lights off. I did not want to see what I was doing to myself; I also didn't want to stop. And I didn't, not until I reached the unpopped kernels at the bottom of the bag.

I didn't just feel full. More like bloated. Disgusted with myself.

The bright clock read 2:50 a.m. *Let this be the last binge of the night*, I prayed.

I hated myself.

Life After Rehab

The above incident happened in my mid-thirties, long after I had finished rehab and left my parents' house. So let me backup a little, to some of the events that led me here.

After the accident, the State of Colorado had charged Nate with vehicular assault and driving under the influence of alcohol (D.U.I.) I suppose the reckless driving and speeding charges (going 70 mph in a 45-mph zone) are part of the vehicular assault? He pleaded guilty to both. He got off pretty lightly in the end, though. Court records showed he was required to attend mental health and alcohol counseling at the Academy. His father, a Three-Star General, flew out to convince Academy officials to keep Nate enrolled. Given it was his senior year, and who he was, it worked.

The military brass also charmed my mother. Nate's father, the general, showered my mom with flowers and favors, such as special seating at football games. The Commandant of Cadets, a general who was in my father's class of 1960, opened his home to my mother and me during the holidays. We even shared Thanksgiving dinner with his family. My mom appreciated these benefits conferred on her. She lived in Colorado Springs with my sponsor, Jan, the entire four months, making daily trips to the hospital. I'm not sure my mother realized that underneath all the niceties, the military was just aiming to keep us quiet.

My dad on the other hand was angry about all the rules broken by the Academy officers that put me in that kind of situation to begin with. Add to that most of the accident was being covered up by the stars (generals) because it was a PR disaster.

I lived through all this in a dream state. I told the DA's office in October of 1983 that Nate should pay some type of consequence for his behavior, even if it included a short jail sentence. Again, in April of 1984, according to a pre-sentence investigation report, I told the DA's office that I felt Nate should receive some type of jail sentence, but not a lot of time. I agreed thirty days in the El Paso County jail would be appropriate. So that is what the state recommended, plus forty-eight hours of community service at his new duty station. The judge deferred the jail sentence.

At this point all I could focus on was rebuilding my life, which demanded all my energy and attention. When I obeyed my dad's orders to join my older sister, Rachel, in Dallas, I lost both the safety of my daily routine in Jackson and my best friend (my mother) - my lifeline. "Move on with your life, you and your mother have gotten too close (co-dependent)," my dad told me.

Too bad for Rachel. I might have looked on the outside like a twenty-year-old, but in truth, I had become a very insecure adolescent. Without my mother, I could hardly function emotionally and mentally. Not exactly the ideal college roomie.

After one semester at Richland Community College, I felt ready to move to a university and take on a normal course load. With no intact internal compass, I did the only thing I could come up with and followed my sister to Southern Methodist University (SMU.)

At SMU sororities and fraternities take center stage in campus life. Looks count for just about everything. My self-esteem nose-dived in record time as I compared myself to the many "flawless" beauties around me. Insecurities I had always carried around now began to dominate my life.

So instead of rebuilding my life, as my parents had mandated, I began to hide out in our townhome. Food and television became my new best friends. Friday nights I had a standing date with the shows *Dallas* and *Dynasty*. I always watched them while eating a Domino's Canadian bacon and mushroom pizza, followed by a half-gallon of Blue Bell Caramel Turtle Fudge ice cream. My version of dinner and a movie. While my sister dated and hung out with friends, I cocooned. Of course, I felt jealous of her. Something was wrong with me, seriously wrong.

When I finally mustered up the courage to see a counselor my senior year at school, I confessed, "My body looks like it has been put through a meat grinder with all the scars I have. Why would anyone ever want to date me?" I hated this post-accident body—which translated to I hated me.

Several decades later I watched the movie *Insomnia* with Al Pacino. Pacino plays a cop on a homicide case in Alaska. After six days without sleep (due to the constant sunlight and his unrelenting emotional demons) he becomes unsure of himself. Spoiler alert: at the end of the movie, he gets shot. As he lay dying, he says to his partner, " I just want to go to sleep. I want to sleep." Then he shuts his eyes for good.

After the car accident I frequently felt like this. I wanted a way to numb the pain, both physical and emotional. In the hospital I had looked forward to surgery because of the blissful nothingness bestowed upon me by anesthesia. Everything would go dark, no feeling, no more pain. I craved it.

Of course, I always paid for it later. When I woke, I would find myself shivering. No matter how many blankets the recovery room nurses piled on me, I could not get warm. A half-awake, half-asleep fog kept me from uttering even the simplest phrase through chattering teeth.

In the years after the crash my life seemed a bit like this after-surgery haze. Eventually I graduated from SMU. But I had not matriculated from my tendency to blindly obey my father's orders. At his insistence, I used money from a small insurance settlement from the accident to purchase his business, Sea Ties, Inc. For three years, from 1987-1990, I lived in Baton Rouge, Louisiana. I ran the business according to my father's instructions, doing my best to make it through each lonely day without falling apart. I had never had a moment of interest in either the product, bungee cords, (yes, you read that right) or in owning a small business. But I knew all about pleasing my parents.

At some point it became too much, even for me. I—gulp—decided to pursue my own interests. I went back to school for a Master's in Public Health - Nutrition. I was searching for an answer to my secret problem of compulsive eating (later defined as binge-eating), something that troubled me even more than the fallout of going against my parents' wishes. "You're so thin," people would say. Little did they know how much food and eating ruled my life. I hoped that becoming a Registered Dietitian (R.D.) would finally help me regain control of the issue.

It didn't. In my thirties, when the opening story of this chapter took place, I was still dealing with binge-eating every day. One doctor diagnosed me with nocturnal sleep-related eating disorder. Over the next decade I began partaking of an extensive medical buffet of doctors and diagnoses (several wrong) and was put on forty-one different drugs during those years trying to help my many different diagnoses. Nothing seemed to work. My body just would not respond. In fact, several of the medications had a paradoxical effect. At one point I was on twelve rounds of antibiotics in a year. By March 2002 I could barely function and took an extended sick leave from my work at the Centers for Disease Control and Prevention (CDC) where I had worked since 1996. My mom came to help me. I took all my drugs and flushed them down the toilet (sorry, ocean, for polluting the water) because I knew these drugs were not the answer for me. Parallel to seeing all these doctors, I was also in individual and group therapy dealing with my issues, learning new skills, and most importantly processing the trauma of my car crash. I constantly wanted this waking and eating behavior to end, and I tried every behavioral strategy imaginable, including locking the refrigerator, all to no avail.

But my advanced degree did carry me into a new world. I took a job at the science-based CDC in Atlanta, Georgia right after the Olympics in 1996, as a Health Communications Specialist in the Division of Nutrition, Physical Activity, and Obesity.

In my new life in Atlanta, I took on a new motto. Even if I never consciously said it to myself in so many words, I set my compass to the phrase, "Safety above all else." I had a secure government job. I bought only big cars, four-door sedans that rode high and had good consumer crash test scores—definitely no convertibles or any type of sports car. My big, three-bedroom house served as my fortress. I even put a curfew on my social life. Staying out past 10 p.m. left me feeling anxious, especially if I found myself around anyone drinking. So, I made a point to come home before then. During this period, I might wake up as many as five times in a single night. Anxiety plagued me, both awake and asleep.

Happiness? I had heard about it; some people even claimed to find it. Joy? Forget it. Life was a matter of survival, not fun. I had learned that the hard way. If I did one thing wrong, God would know, even if no one else did, and come for me.

This attitude took its toll on me. No wonder I sought comfort and release at the bottom of a pint of Ben and Jerry's. I might know all about the government's recommendations for a healthy meal; however, my work as a dietitian had taught me not a single thing about how to recover from serious trauma.

Still, I went about my life pretending like nothing had ever happened to me. At least that's how I thought of it. Any savvy onlooker could have made a clear connection between the trauma I had endured and the kind of life I had created for myself. To me, though, it just occurred like "This is the way I am." I tried my best not to bring up the accident with other people. Most days I tried my best not to even think about it, which didn't work.

I was doing my very best to live. My body, on the other hand, was constantly focused on trying not to die.

How ironic. Already I had faced death. I knew it held no suffering. But that didn't stop my body from pushing against it all the time. The gap between my conscious desire to create a life beyond the trauma of the accident and the forgotten experiences still held by my body and mind monopolized me.

Trauma and Memory

One of the leading authors and researchers on post-traumatic stress is psychiatrist Dr. Bessel van der Kolk. In his book, *The Body Keeps the Score*, he states, "Traumatized people simultaneously remember too little and too much."

Under normal circumstances, the rational part of the brain (frontal lobe) works together with the emotional (limbic) area to create a coherent understanding of what's happening around you. Your husband walks in the front door, and you tell yourself, he's been at work all day and now he's back home. It may or may not be true. For all you know, he could have spent the day playing hooky. Still, your mind has created a clear story for what the eyes have shown the brain, based on past experience.

To create a vivid, lasting memory, though, you usually need to add some emotion to the mix. Witness a violent car crash, and you're likely to have a very clear memory of what you saw. The amygdalae, a pair of almond-shaped structures located deep in the brain, link your emotional perception of what happened with the details of what you saw. It tells your hippocampus, "Hey, this event needs to go into a part of the brain where we can get it back again so we can avoid repeating it." Adrenaline helps this process along. It turns up the volume on your brain's memory system.

But adrenaline can make you vividly aware and alert only up to a point. Once a high amount of adrenaline is released, the brain can no longer keep things straight. The frontal lobe shuts down, including the area needed to put feelings into words. This rational part of the brain gets out of sync with the emotional (limbic) system. Areas of the brain that you need for storing and integrating new information—the hippocampus and the thalamus, for instance—go offline. You might retain fragments of a highly traumatic event, but often not everything.

In some cases, you might remember nothing. That's when your system creates a repressed memory. Your brain did record what happened. You just can't access a coherent memory of it.

Before I go any further on this topic, let me mention that some scientists and even psychologists say that repressed memory doesn't exist. Human memory doesn't work this way, they insist. They point to memory studies where people have had a false memory "implanted" by the researcher, one the participant believed to be their own.

But this scientific argument against the notion of repressed memory overlooks a very important detail. Truth is, you can't create trauma in a lab—or at least you should not! Scientists have no way to study, in white coats with clinical reserve, the way the brain functions when trauma is happening.

Because of this constraint, Bessel van der Kolk turned to practical sources to understand trauma when he first began to address it with his patients. Among other things, he explored early research on medical hysteria.

Maybe you've heard of hysterical blindness, just one example of medical hysteria. A person with this condition has eyes that function, physically speaking—at least in theory. Doctors can detect no anatomical problems with the eyes. Yet the person cannot see.

Medical hysteria received a lot of attention in the late 1800s when Dr. Pierre Janet devoted his lab to the study of the phenomenon. As a psychotherapist, his interest was in the field of dissociation and traumatic memory. He is one of the founding fathers of psychology. In 1889, he published an article about the case of Lelog, a man who survived a traffic accident involving a horse-drawn cart. The man had passed out during the accident but sustained no major injuries. Yet, afterwards, Lelog could not walk. Doctors could find no neurological or anatomical reasons for the loss of his leg function. In working with Lelog, however, Janet learned that just before Lelog passed out he had seen the wheels of the cart moving in his direction. Lelog had strongly believed that the cart would run over his legs. He had no memory of the accident itself.

In other words, Lelog's body was telling the story of what had happened. That is, his body was expressing, without words, his mind's version of what had happened, not what had actually occurred.

This story illustrates so clearly the way traumatic memories are stored in, or you might say, expressed through the body. (I found this story, by the way, in Bessel van der Kolk's *The Body Keeps the Score,* if you'd like to read more.)

Speak to any psychotherapist who has successfully treated severely traumatized patients, and you're bound to hear that repressed memory has surfaced in their treatments.

I'm the perfect example. Like Lelog, I was carrying in my conscious memory a blank space where the accident had happened. Yet my body had not forgotten. In the next chapter, I'll give more details on how that played out for me.

Suppression

Suppression happens when we consciously push down our unwanted feelings, thoughts, memories, emotions, fantasies, etc. We do this with things that bring too much pain—shame, anger, blame, grief, sadness, you name it—into our awareness. When a thought or feeling conflicts with our values or beliefs, we can suppress it. In both instances, we tell ourselves, let's not go there.

In the long run, suppression, a more voluntary version of repression, takes its toll on body and mind. Neuropeptides, those messenger molecules I discussed in the last chapter, should have room to wash through your system with their emotional messages. When you don't allow them to, they stay lodged in your mind-body system. You drag them around like dead weight.

To illustrate, think of the stress you feel every time you look at that messy pile of junk in your garage/kitchen/pantry, etc. I'm talking about the room, shelf, or closet you know you should organize, but you never do. Instead, you throw, cram, or shove things in there then close the door. You never want to spend any time there, either. It's such a dump. If you ever end up moving, you'll either have to shove all that stuff in boxes and drag it around or finally deal with it all.

That happens inside the body with suppressed emotions and memories, too. You can see how this cycle can create disease in the body. It can carry around your suppressed memories, yes, but only to a point. When they become too much, you pay the price. Physical symptoms express what you have not.

We have a million strategies to keep the past suppressed. If you love coffee, you know what I'm talking about. Six fifteen a.m. comes, and you have only the dimmest recollection of how that coffee mug, full of hot coffee, got into your hands. Caffeine, the world's most commonly ingested psychoactive substance, gives your brain a little dopamine hit. Take a sip, and—wow, says the brain. That's really nice. Ice cream, popcorn, fatty foods like cheese, sugar—they all work the same magic on your brain.

You can see how physiology and psychology loop back and forth when it comes to suppression. That feeling of dread that washes over you at the sound of your alarm—how you hate your job!—needs a remedy. Time for coffee. Dopamine, please, to blunt the emotion.

On the downside of the dopamine rollercoaster, you crash. So, you have to go back for more coffee (ice cream, cheese, etc.). Only this time, your brain has said, wait a minute. The last time caffeine came in, it came at me just a little too hard. I'm not used to having so much pleasure all at once! I'd better thin down the number of dopamine receptors so I won't take such a hit next time.

Now you need more coffee to get the same results you did the first time. Your brain thins down the receptors further, so you drink more. Then still more. Sooner or later, caffeine addiction has taken up residence in your system.

Our culture offers so many ways to distract from the stuff we don't want to feel. In the example at the opening of this chapter, I was using food. But you can numb out with anything. Social media, video games, Netflix/Hulu/Amazon, or any other platform that encourages binge watching. Dare I even mention where we're heading with virtual reality? Of course, you don't have to use entertainment. You can avoid looking deeper at yourself through something like overwork or over committing yourself just as easily.

Bottom line: Suppression costs you. You've pushed stuff down to avoid your feelings. So instead of feeling the pain fully once, you suffer from it every day. Maybe that suffering seems worth the price—until it turns into something like cancer.

Swiss psychiatrist Carl Jung who created Jungian psychology used the word "shadow" to talk about suppression. Aspects of your experience you've put out of your awareness you have put into your shadow.

Projection

Another side effect of suppression comes in the form of defensive projection. When you can't face something in yourself, and you suppress it, you end up displacing it onto other people.

Think of the school bully who beats up on the weakest kid in his class. At home, the bully's father beats on him, often without warning, which leaves the boy feeling vulnerable and helpless. Because he can't afford to feel those feelings of insecurity, he projects them onto an outside target. For a moment, he feels powerful again.

You don't have to be a bully to project, though. We project our feelings all the time. "She must be so lonely," you say to yourself about a woman sitting alone at lunch. Perhaps the woman is enjoying every minute of her meal; this is the one time in her week when she gets time alone. You, however, struggle with loneliness and do everything you can to avoid solo time. You have projected those feelings onto her.

Anything in yourself that you've suppressed you will project onto others, plain and simple.

No wonder so many of us struggle in our relationships. You can't see the other person clearly if you are constantly looking at him or her through the many layers of your own unresolved issues.

A Moment of Clarity

Tears.

At first just a few fat drops, one rolling after the next in dignified procession.

It's Christmas 2020. The pandemic has pushed me to create a makeshift "gym" at home, where I do yoga alone now. But I can barely hold this pose. Grief pushes and swells against my ribs, tender and sore.

Then the dam bursts. Sobs break through me in heaving waves. Pure emotion, no stories attached.

Where is all this grief coming from?

Yes, I get that the whole world is doing Christmas differently this year, loved ones not physically together. But that's not really it, not entirely.

My mind flashes to the friendship that went south earlier this year. I had relied on her like a sister for over two decades. But nope. Not the reason for these tears.

Then I think of my parents in Australia. We haven't spoken in two years as I needed to set a boundary to continue my healing journey. This year's the first one with neither of us sending a card or calling for Christmas. Huh-uh. That's not it either.

Then it hits me. This grief, it's about God. And me.

With this, the tears begin to slow. I'm sitting up now with understanding washing through me.

In my heart, I had bought The Lie: We'll always be here for each other. We'll work through anything that comes up for us. So desperately I wanted unconditional love and acceptance from my mother, my father, my best friend that I had pinned all my hopes on phrases like these.

Now they are gone.

And I grieve because... well, not because they're gone. But because I was looking to them to be there for me instead of me being there for me.

I am the only one who is going to be here in every moment of my entire life. It's my job—not theirs—to show up for myself. I remember that I am really one with God. In this relationship, I am never abandoned.

The tears have stopped now, replaced with the warm glow of satisfaction. I feel my soul, in a way I haven't in decades.

Time for a child's pose.

Patterns

Patterns drive us.

Take a look at the center of a sunflower and you'll see the Fibonacci Sequence, a mathematical pattern named in the 1200s after Leonardo Fibonacci, who first pointed to it. If you remember back to math class, each number in the sequence is the sum of the previous two numbers, so, 1, 2, 3, 5, 8, 13, 21, 34, 55, 89, 144, etc.

In the human body-mind system, patterns like this one not only organize the body's functioning, but they also shape how we move through the world. Think of your routines. When you wake you are probably not going through a mental rehearsal such as, "Now it's time to brush my teeth. Pick up the toothbrush. Put on the toothpaste. Turn on the water..." If your pattern is to wake up and brush your teeth first thing, then you have probably found yourself, at some point or other, groggily rinsing toothpaste from your mouth without even realizing you had picked up the brush. You have performed this particular sequence of actions so many times that it has gotten neurologically wired, so to speak.

"Neurons that fire together, wire together." Dr. Donald Hebb, a Canadian psychologist specializing in neuropsychology, first made this pronouncement back in 1949. It has since become a mainstay in modern psychology's understanding of the way the brain functions. The more often you do an action, the more deeply connected its related neurons become.

It helps explain how unconscious patterns of thought and behavior form. Not all of your patterns are negative, of course. You can create a healthy pattern of exercising daily, for instance. Many patterns, however, remain unconscious until you make an effort to see them. Everything I've shared so far about the human mind-body system—identity, limiting beliefs, trauma, suppression, projection, physical systems, and structures—conspires in the formation of your patterns.

Have you ever found yourself saying something in the exact same words and the exact same tone as your mother or father always did? I have a friend who went to college with a maternal cousin. The two cousins did not grow up in the same town and usually only saw each other a few times a year. Then in college, my friend served on the board of a club with one of her cousin's best friends. My friend had not really spent any time with this friend of her cousin. Yet her cousin's friend could not stop commenting on how much my friend sounded like her cousin. "You use the same expressions as your cousin. Ones I have never heard in my life. You even use the same inflection. Sometimes I have this moment of confusion because I think I'm talking to her and not to you, even though you two look nothing alike." My friend had taken on the patterns of speech of her mother, which her mother and her mother's sister had both learned in childhood. The patterns were passed down to the daughters of both sisters. If my friend's simple speech habits so closely resembled her mother's, imagine all the other patterns my friend had picked up from her mom along the way.

Now take a look at my life. Eating during a lonely time created a chemical response in my body. These chemicals did offer some degree of temporary comfort, in the form of dopamine, along with a reminder of special moments from my childhood. Since I couldn't figure out another way to soothe myself, I began to turn to food habitually. Dopamine reinforced this choice. The rare treat of ice cream and TV I had known as a kid eventually mushroomed into a pattern of binge eating. My whole life eventually revolved around it. Even the profession I chose arose from this pattern.

Of course, your patterns don't have to be rooted in an abusive practice to take on the quality of addiction. My own pattern of seeking safety in all things offers one example of what I mean. This pattern overshadowed every aspect of my life. An emotional pattern of anxiety underscored it. This duo - anxiety/seek safety, anxiety/seek safety - had arisen from the many things my body-mind had endured that I had not yet integrated.

What I've shared from this era of my life illustrates the way that most of the time the brain functions on autopilot, with the unconscious mind running anywhere from 95 to 99% of your choices. Only a minute fraction of the information bubbling around in your body-mind ever rises into your conscious awareness. Like it or not, the unconscious mind runs your life—most of it programmed into its patterns by the ripe old age of six.

If you want to see your future, you don't need to consult a psychic. Just look at yesterday. Last month. Last year. Your patterns will continue just as they have—unless you find a way to interrupt them.

I'm not claiming this is easy. Ask any alcoholic who's been sober for decades if the craving for alcohol has gone away. One woman I know put it this way. When questioned, after more than thirty years without a drink, about why she did not enjoy just one glass of wine every now and then, she answered, "Who wants just one?"

How frustrating it feels to yearn to free yourself of negative patterns. You can hate yourself for going back to the abusive ex, or for eating another potato chip, or spending more money than you have again this month. Or maybe you just want to stop the habit of something like pleasing other people or ending up with the wrong kind of guy. Anyone else besides me ever wanted to be able to go to the doctor to have an unhealthy pattern surgically removed?

But patterns are precious clues; a trail of breadcrumbs left in the forest. By examining your patterns, you can find your way back home to who you were before trauma and habit had their ways with you.

Are you ready?

One reason we fear death: We fear the feelings we've buried.

In the day to day, we can be distracted. Pretend. Push aside. To deny what we feel and avoid vulnerability, we project. And we allow our patterns to run the show.

But death offers no such luxury. Often, the pain that precedes death isn't physical, either. Rather, it comes in the shape of regret for the things we did or did not do.

Why didn't I...? How come I...? What if I had only...? We see more clearly the negative habits that sucked away our life force.

In my case, I didn't even have time for the kind of reflection that is so often a part of the process of dying. All that came for me after the crash. To deal with my death, I had to learn to live.

And that's true for all of us. A good death begins now, today. The more courage you muster to allow the unresolved to surface, the easier it becomes to face what awaits you next.

CHAPTER 7: THE BODY REMEMBERS

Lesson 7: *We are not judged.*[*]

Time Travel

It starts like any other day. One minute I am waiting in line at Starbucks for my morning caffeine fix, the next, I am coming unglued. I take a sip of my soy latte and find I am no longer in my navy-blue Acura Legend on my way to work at the CDC. Instead, I find myself back in Colorado, nineteen years before, in that 1965 Rally Red Corvette convertible.

I'm sitting in the passenger seat. I have propped my right foot on the dashboard, sporting my new Adidas sneaker, with my left knee bent and left foot resting on my right knee. A triangle. I'm leaning back in the bucket seat with the wind blowing in my face, staring into the brilliant afterglow of a fading sunset over the Rockies. I glance over to the speedometer. The needle is moving further and further to the right. Wait, we're gaining too much speed! We're going too fast for this curve!

When I look down again, I see the Starbucks cup in my hand is shaking. No, my entire body is shaking. I think, "Better start cutting down on caffeine." But then I realize this isn't just an increase in my heartbeat. I am feeling overwhelming anxiety, working up to a full-on panic attack. I pull to the shoulder of the road, take a deep breath, then decide to bypass my office and head straight for my doctor.

Dr. Kenneth West has been my chiropractor for years. Since he does bodywork, I hope he will know why my body is shaking so badly and can help me. When his receptionist tells me he is booked for the day, I can hear a faint note of panic in my voice as I explain it is an emergency. I tell her I am willing to wait as long as I need to until she can

* Source: https://mcusercontent.com/6aeb61681f6c311e999fff730/files/5070a118-63b3-4ac3-87f4-08b4f5d6e2e0/2020_IANDS_Annual_Report.01.pdf pg. 15

fit me in, please. Then I install myself in a waiting room chair, my body still quivering.

Luckily, my moment comes. As soon as Dr. West walks into my exam room, I blurt out what is happening to me. He assures me I will be okay. Repressed memories of the car crash, Dr. West explains, are rising to the surface.

Great, I think sourly. Why now, so many years later? Is it possible Dr. West doesn't really understand my situation?

But on his exam table, I start remembering more. I am cringing inside, fidgeting like I need to get up. When will it finally be over? I have no idea what is trying to happen, only that I don't want to let it happen.

But here is Dr. West, reminding me I am safe with him, as he has proven to me so many times. He will stay with me through this; he reassures me. As he soothes me, I feel myself relax into the pressing memory.

The red Corvette is waiting for us in front of the little shack. Wow, Nate orders us two beers each and pays for them, then pulls out a pack of cigarettes. Not even going to think about what Dad would do if he knew. I mean, Nate is cute, but his roommate is who I have a crush on, and as a people pleaser I want him to like me. Besides, I'm old enough now to figure things out for myself.

I slide into the passenger side feeling relaxed and carefree. A vague sense of pressure does push on me from some remote corner of my mind—we have to get back before curfew, and I've got to finish that horrible English paper. To hell with all that, for once, I'm going to enjoy myself.

Nate suggests we stop and watch the sunset. As he pulls over, he turns off the engine and reaches over to touch my thigh. Suddenly I'm hyper-aware. The dashboard comes into sharp focus. I notice the shape of his hand resting on my thigh. I'm wearing khaki shorts and an Izod polo shirt with teal stripes.

Nate reaches over trying to kiss me. He has soft, wet lips, loose and open. But then his hands are, well, just about everywhere. He's crossed into the red zone already. This is too fast. I get scared about where it will lead and interrupt him.

"We must get back to the Academy. We're going to be late, and I'll be in big trouble."

"C'mon, relax," he says, "It's no big deal."

With that, the memory fades, and I find myself in the exam room again. I am breathing hard, confused. I had been somewhere far away. Sensing I had finished a cycle, Dr. West shifts his hands to a new set of acupressure points as I hear a sigh leave my body.

I am spinning around insanely fast, like those tilt-a-whirl carnival rides, grabbing the side of the car door. I scream as my side of the car smashes head-on into... something, what is it? I realize I can't stop anything, and my voice fades. I fly out of my seat, through the windshield.

Around me, glass is shattering like splatter paint. I feel pieces of it cutting into my thighs and legs. God, this hurts! And then something slices my left foot, bad. I try to shield my face with my hand, my mouth wide open under it. Then I'm in the air for what feels like forever. When I finally hit the ground, I understand that I am going to die.

My mind freezes. I scream, "OH, my God, help me!" Then I have one final thought, "I'm not going to make it."

Then that's it. The end of my treatment with Dr. West. Reliving that moment of hanging in midair just before death had terrified me.

I go straight home from Dr. West's office feeling completely rung out. I had accessed a whole new chunk of the memory of the accident, but I know it wasn't everything. Whatever hadn't surfaced yet still sits like a lump of wet cotton in my throat. I can't stand this irritating feeling of being left hanging, not knowing when, or if, the rest of the memory will return. I have no idea what triggered this sudden recall of the crash almost two decades later, but clearly something did.

That night I made a point to sleep in my guest bedroom since it is smaller and feels safer to me. I crawled into the queen-size waterbed, my body drifting toward sleep like a raft unmoored. In this half-awake state, more of the memory comes back to me.

When we pull back onto the road, Nate reaches his free right hand to grab my left thigh again as he pushes hard on the gas.

"No," I protested. "I'm not going there. We have to get back."

He is mad at me now, accelerating. The speedometer's needle climbs—50, 60, 70 mph. He jerks his hand angrily back to the steering wheel just as we get to a curve in the road.

Now the car is fishtailing, and I scream. My body is smashing into the side of the passenger door. Then I'm hanging in mid-air, shrieking in horror. First, I free fall for an eternity, then I crash hard into the ground. Blackness.

In the next instant, intensely bright white lights flood me. They are almost blinding, except not exactly, since they also feel warm and comforting. They wrap around me, soft and safe. I float upward. When I look down, I see my body lying in the ditch, mangled and lifeless.

Suddenly, a deep voice calls. I look around for the speaker but find no one. Then I see a fuzzy shape. It reminds me of Casper the Friendly Ghost, but with a vaguer outline than that. The shape calls me. I'm not sure how I know, but the shape is a "he," a male presence. He wants me to follow him further into the light.

Without hesitation, I do. Upward I float, still immersed in the soothing, beautiful light. How incredible this feels, moving around without the weight of a body to drag me down. Or maybe this is a different kind of body. This is so far beyond happiness. I'm in rapture.

Then I notice other Beings like my host, lots of them. They all seem to know one another. I am not sure how they communicate with each other, but somehow, I understand them.

I hear one Being communicate, "I really want to help them, but they have to ask for our help first. I am not going to interfere unless asked."

Then the Being who has been guiding me communicates, "Nicole, your mission is to tell people not to be afraid of death."

With this, I realize in horror that they are not going to let me stay here. I'm being sent back down there! Back to the pain and the gruesomely ruined body. Nothing but hurt!

"No!"

The next day, I called in sick. But it will take decades for me to puzzle through what I had just experienced.

The Body Remembers

Before these chunks of memory returned, I had tried in vain to reconstruct how I could have been sitting in the car before impact. What body position could have possibly caused my left foot to be almost completely sliced off? Had I been leaning back in my seat with both feet on the dashboard? But that still didn't fit with the injuries I sustained.

Only with the flashbacks did the pieces of that mystery fall into place. The triangle shape of my left foot on my right thigh, left knee bent, finally made sense of why just one foot had been cut the way it had and why the insides of both thighs and my vagina had fourth degree lacerations.

The way that detail lined up with what I already knew had happened to my body lent credibility to all the other vivid shards of the memory that had come back to me.

For the first time I was realizing that I had refused a sexual advance and almost died for it. Just as my foot had been severed by the angle of impact, my trust in men had been mangled and almost lost completely. Since the accident, my relationships with men have been terrible. Only now could I see why.

It didn't stop there. Along with this excruciating new awareness, I was also holding an incredible memory of life on the other side of death. That place, the place where what many people call "angels" had communicated with me and with each other, looked nothing like the mansions in the sky I had learned about in childhood. No streets paved with gold, no St. Peter ushering me through pearly gates. A kindly old man with a white beard had not shown up to fill me in on my test scores in the exam I had been calling my life.

And yet I had experienced heaven. I had known myself in a state that not even the word bliss can describe. In that place, that state, I was not standing before God. I was God.

Somehow, I would have to make sense of these two worlds.

Bringing Coherence: Remembering

Why did I suddenly remember?

At that time in my life, I was partaking of a host of different healing modalities. I saw my chiropractor regularly and had other forms of body work. I was also working with a psychotherapist to make sense of tangled emotions. And I attended a supportive church, one with a life-affirming approach to spirituality.

In other words, I had a lot of support. This network of caring hadn't fallen from the sky, mind you. I had worked to find both individuals and communities where I received care and compassion. If I had instead hidden out in the familiar religion of my childhood, with its many rules and distrust in things like therapy or even Reiki (hands on energy healing), I might have lived the remainder of my life without conscious access to what had happened to me.

To further illuminate what I mean, here's a case study from the French doctor I mentioned in the last chapter, Janet, author of *The Body Keeps the Score*. One of Janet's patients had been nursing her dying mother while also working full-time to provide financially for her mother and her alcoholic father. When her mother died, she tried for hours to revive the body. At one point, she even attempted to force medicine down her departed mother's throat while her drunken father lay passed out in a corner of the same room.

When her aunt arrived to help with funeral preparations, the daughter still did not believe her mother had died. She only attended the funeral when made to do so and then laughed loudly through the service.

One especially poignant aspect of this woman's story happened multiple times a week. At the sight of a bed, she would enter a trance state. For hours she would care for someone only she could see. Instead of remembering what had happened, she was reenacting it.

Janet began the woman's treatment. Months of hypnotherapy eventually brought her to a state of mind where she could again remember. Instead of re-enacting the story, she began to retell it. In retelling it, she experienced the powerful grief she had buried. With this, her compulsion to care for an invisible person at the sight of a bed resolved itself.

My parents might say that this case study proves that therapy is for crazy people like this lady. I beg to differ. I myself have lived with the impact of unresolved, unremembered trauma. Virtually all of us do to varying degrees.

In the last chapter, I shared some details about how traumatic experiences can alter the brain's memory functions. Too much adrenaline can force the various brain structures needed to create a coherent memory offline.

When this happens, the body-mind needs expert assistance to shift this pattern and pull fragmented pieces of the past into a coherent whole. With the right support, the emotional (limbic system) and rational (frontal lobe) parts of the brain can once again begin to work together as a team, producing a clear coherent narrative about what happened during a traumatic event.

This is how we remember ourselves.

As my buried memories surfaced, I found myself at the beginning of a positive new chapter in my life. I still had a long road to walk in my recovery, including the tears I would shed as I lived with the pain the memories brought with it—once numbed out by forgetfulness, but now right in my face. I had bottled those tears inside me for so long; letting them out was truly liberating.

Possibly the most important realization for me was on Feb. 16, 2022, when I woke up with a migraine from hell and my stomach belching uncontrollably. What in the world?

My husband and I used Neuro Emotional Technique (NET) to review what was coming up for me – the core of my shame. I finally was realizing Nate had killed me, and I had nothing to do with that. My body was just now, after all those years, able to embody the truth, and oh my did I feel all the emotions that went with it for the next hour. NET helped identify them as bad memories (indeed), mortification, panic, emotional repression, depression, and forgetfulness (not wanting to think or feel it). It was like the Hoover Dam burst and it all flooded over me. I will tell you, I had to take an anti-anxiety drug for this one. Releasing and realizing this truth has changed my story, hence my life. I have now totally freed myself of any blame or shame that I was in any way responsible for Nate crashing his car. I looked at my husband and said, "Why was I never able to connect these dots before?" It seemed so obvious – I wasn't driving, so end of story, right? But the POWER my parents held over me ran my life.

You see, I really believed I was somehow to blame for the accident because my parents said so – I had broken Dad's rules. So, when Nate pled guilty to vehicular assault it could have easily been vehicular homicide - dangerous driving causing death. Yet, because I had no memory of the crash for nineteen years and I was so insecure, I believed anything my parents said - it must be the truth. AND, they have never recanted it or apologized for any of this. When my memory did return it didn't compute that part, probably because I was so mortified of what it would reveal – the NDE and being sexually assaulted.

Since that revelation I am different. I have dealt with my anger toward both my parents for creating a lie that has caused me immense pain and suffering. I am reminded of the quote, "You shall know the truth and the truth shall set you free." I am finally free of my parents and the old concept of a vengeful God whom I had displeased.

Spiritual Amnesia

What surprised and amazed me most from the memory was my lucid recall of my time on the other side of death. Was it really possible I had ventured beyond this world? I wanted to doubt myself, to disbelieve what I had experienced. Yet I couldn't shake the memory of that place. In many ways, the world beyond my body felt more real than this one.

You may remember what I shared in the last chapter about repression. We repress memories when we feel unsafe, such as when the event so overwhelms us that it seems life-threatening, or when a traumatic event occurs at an age before we have the cognitive ability to process it.

In this case, my experience of death could only be described as positive, not traumatic. Why hadn't I retained a conscious memory of that experience?

For one thing, my body-mind had a lot to contend with just after the accident. One surgery followed another, so that I lived in a haze of numbing drugs. I could barely hold on to a single thought at the time. Physically, I had no resources to help me retain the NDE in my conscious memory.

The emotional climate of my life also played a role. As I've shared at length, I lived in the shadow of a father so rigid and rule-enforcing that fear filled me most of the time. Long before I even left home for the Academy, anxiety overshadowed my life. According to experts at the University of Minnesota, fear can inhibit the creation of long-term memories and even damage the hippocampus, the region of the brain that houses memory. With this, the brain's ability to respond to situations gets short-circuited. A person in this condition lives with constant feelings of anxiety. "Constant feelings of anxiety" sounds like an accurate description of my childhood and life at the Academy. Ironically, I only felt safe in a state of fear.

On top of that, I had come back to a world where I could find myself sternly corrected or even severely punished for sharing what I had experienced out of my body. Like a child, I had to rely completely on my father and mother just to survive. Forget about talking to them, the only people I had contact with on a regular basis, about the realm I had encountered beyond death. To be honest, all those years of Sunday School and hell-fire-brimstone preachers had me so spooked that I could not even dare to admit to myself anything that would deviate from my parents' worldview.

Even with all of this, though, I never fully forgot the NDE in those years after the crash. From day one in the hospital, I remembered seeing bright, white lights, and these words only vaguely hint at the experience. I did not have the eyes of this physical body to see with, nor the limitations that eyes impose. "Brilliance" or "radiance" or "effulgence" might come a little closer to describing that light. In fact, references to white lights appear again and again in accounts of NDEs around the world. They are one of the most common elements of NDE accounts across all races, religions, and cultures.

Deep down I think I always knew that I had a spiritual encounter after the crash. Though my logical mind kept questioning it. When I trained as a scientist in my post college work and days at the CDC, I learned to question everything, especially anything I could not quantify in a lab. Oh, and myself, too. I especially learned to question myself. All of that made it easy for me to forget what had happened.

This condition of forgetfulness afflicts all of us, though. Everyone existed in that state of oneness and peace beyond the body before we came here. Yet very few of us can remember being there. When someone who retains a memory of it tells us about it, we usually doubt the account. The influences of family, culture, religion, unresolved trauma, our patterns, and cherished identities—all of these can get in the way of remembrance.

I call this spiritual amnesia. If you're human, you most likely suffer from it. It happens when you forget who you truly are: God taking a walkabout in a physical body.

You and I are both infinite, powerful, limitless, radiant, glorious, and eternal. If it doesn't seem that way to you, then you're just suffering from a case of spiritual amnesia. Piled with layers of other people's crud, you can no longer see yourself clearly. Because you've normalized it, forgetting seems like reality. Waking up from this forgetfulness is the main task we all face.

Luckily, none of us can fully sever our ties with the God Self within. Though the outer personality and the body might forget, this great Self always keeps the flames of remembrance burning.

A Word on Spiritual Bypass

I've shared a lot in this book about the spiritual dimension of our lives. Even now I'm telling you that the aim of the game here is to remember who we are as Spirit, while living a physical life.

Now I want to point out one pitfall that comes with all this spiritual talk: Spiritual bypass.

Spiritual bypass happens when we use spirituality—at least a mental understanding of it—to avoid painful feelings. No matter how "enlightened" your beliefs are, you can still fall prey to this tendency. (I think the more enlightened you think you are, the more likely you are to practice spiritual bypass.)

If you've spent time in a spiritual community, you have probably felt the sting of spiritual bypass perpetrated on you by someone else. A friend of mine was just telling me about an interaction she recently had with another woman. The woman asked her how a visit to her parents had gone. "Rough," my friend confessed. She shared how she had lost her temper with her father. The other woman's response? Something along the lines of, "Well, you know you shouldn't react to him that way because he's just unconscious."

Gross. The last thing my friend needed was a lecture on how she should have done things differently in that situation. She was already beating herself up over it. Besides that, my friend had not come looking for any advice. She didn't bring up the topic in the first place and felt blindsided by the holier-than-thou sermonette.

I'm guessing you also hate to have this kind of smug act played out on you. But do you realize it when you're doing it to yourself? Have you ever caught yourself saying something to yourself like, "I shouldn't feel sad right now? I should be happy. I am a child of God." Anytime you find that word "should" in combination with spiritual platitudes, you've probably fallen into spiritual bypass.

With everything I shared in the last chapter about the cost of suppression and repression, I hope you can see the value in becoming aware of spiritual bypass in yourself. It's just another wolf-in-sheep's-clothing scenario. Suppression wearing a clever mask. Adding the word "God," or some other spiritual jargon, to your self-talk doesn't make it genuinely holy.

But wait, you may be saying. Didn't you just tell me I should wake up to the fact that I'm a spiritual being having a physical experience? Aren't I supposed to replace the habit of forgetting my true self with remembrance of my God Self? How does spiritual bypass fit in with all that?

Well, think about the process of life on planet earth. You came here as a perfect being. Then your family took you home from the hospital. From then on—and okay, before that, in the womb—they started dumping stuff on top of you. You had some traumatic experiences along the way, too. Pretty soon you found yourself walking around under layers and layers of stuff that is not you. It's like wearing too many coats all the time. Whenever you look in the mirror, you only see the coats. You forget what the real you looks like.

You can only remedy the problem in one way. You have to take off the coats.

To do that, you first have to become aware that they are there. You can't keep playing Pollyanna and acting like everything's hunky-dory if it's not. This part of the process usually brings up pain.

In my own story, I experienced an enormous amount of hurt when the memory of the accident resurfaced. Imagine the rage I felt when I realized a drunk man had nearly killed me after trying to get down my pants. But by remembering it, I was taking off a layer of the crud. If I couldn't see it and feel all the feelings that it invoked in me, I couldn't release it. The pain I had numbed out had never left my system; only by feeling it fully, without resisting, did I give it an exit route.

Here's how I talk myself through something like this when I remember. I invite the pain in fully—without becoming that pain.

Feeling the pain, without bathing in it and identifying with it, actually keeps you anchored in the reality beyond all the pain. I like the analogy of the blue sky and clouds. Pain—the clouds—simply pass through the larger blue sky of who you truly are, which does not change.

Panic

I glance around the small exam room. Ragged medical posters—anatomy, health advice—line nondescript beige walls. The scent of hospital-grade sanitizer lingers in the air.

It's late July 2021. I've waited in hundreds of rooms like this one over the past three decades. Today I'm here for a fairly routine treatment. About seven weeks ago, I sprained my right knee, and it still hurts to walk on it.

Sean, my new physician's assistant, explains that I have a cyst and possibly also some torn cartilage. I can get a cortisone shot or an MRI.

No question. I want the pain gone now, so, of course, I choose the shot. In my life I've had more shots than I can count. This will be the first of this kind, but how different can it be?

When I see the metal tray covered in blue paper, I start to question my choice. "Is this like a vaccine?" I ask. A little quiver of nervousness wobbles through my words.

But I don't really hear Sean's answer. He's pulled off the tray's paper cover, and my heartbeat has jumped up another few notches. A glass syringe, vials of clear fluids, some kind of staple-gun looking contraption, and, and ... a HUGE needle!

From somewhere far away, Sean tells me he is going to numb my knee first. "Yes," I hear myself answer, with the strange sensation that someone other than me said the word.

Bang! Bang! Ouch! The staple gun thingy really hurts.

Now the walls are closing in around me. I lose peripheral vision. I can feel myself panting, barely able to breathe.

"Nicole? Nicole, are you okay?"

A voice from somewhere far away is talking. Is that my name I hear?

I mean to answer the voice with something like, not sure, or give me a minute and I will be. But no words come out.

"Are you okay?" the voice asks again.

Now I can't swallow. "I don't think so," I half-whisper.

"I haven't even given you the shot," the voice answers me.

And then it arrives. A Full. Blown. Panic. Attack.

A call goes out, "Get a nurse in here, STAT."

Then Sean is talking to me again. "Do I need to call an ambulance? Do you need to go to the E.R.?"

"No, no, I need my husband." Somehow, I manage, with wildly shaking hands, to dial his number. He knows the drill. Just as soon as he can he'll be here with my Xanax, which, when changing purses in a hurry, I had forgotten. Always keeping my migraine and anxiety medications with me is a rule I live by, except that day.

My vision has blurred. Two new indistinct figures have come into the room. Nurses. One brings water. I tried taking a drink. Then I get grape juice. Breathe, focus, sip. Breathe, focus, sip.

"The color of the wall. Focus on the color of the wall," I tell myself. "Beige. It is beige." My body is shaking. Endlessly it shakes. I clutch the nurse's hand as if I'm drowning and she's a life raft.

Finally, Paul has come. He had to Uber here, and an hour has passed since the attack started. After I take the double dose of Xanax, our routine starts. We've been to the land of anxiety and panic attacks before.

First, Paul starts warming me up, rubbing my hands, feet, arms. Through chattering teeth, I tell him I have to pee so bad, but I can't stand up. Paul grabs the trash can and says, "Go for it."

I do.

Ever so slowly I start making out the table in the room, then the window. I need to look outside. The tree just past this room gets my full focus. "Breathe. Breathe." Gradually the rest of the outdoor scene is clear. My side vision is coming back now, too. The Xanax is kicking in; my body is calming. Strange the way some doctors' offices cannot give you a Xanax but can offer you a trip to the ER.

Sean has been popping in and out for the last two hours to check on me. This time when his head appears I say to him and my nurses, "I know what this is."

I begin to describe that day in the hospital, so many years ago. My lungs were filling up with fluid and I could not breathe. Dr. Stewart had drained my lungs from my backside with the biggest needle I had ever seen. No good, though. My lungs filled up all over again. So here came the needle a second time. But my lungs just refilled.

I couldn't understand what was happening. Why couldn't I breathe? I thought the doctors were causing it, giving me some kind of treatment but refusing the oxygen I needed to get through it.

Actually, I *was* drowning. Literally.

Then Dr. Stewart pushed a drug, a diuretic, into my IV and I proceeded to pee off three quarts of fluid. Finally, I could breathe. My body had been in a massive fluid overload. If not for the diuretic, I would have suffocated from within.

As I finish telling the story, my body has settled enough that I can finally go home. Two full hours have passed. Paul and I leave the little room. I have to pee again. Paul helps me to the bathroom. Then I'm limping through the corridors, leaning on Paul's shoulders.

I end up spending the weekend on the couch, completely wiped out. In a few weeks, I'll be back—this time for the MRI.

Traumatic Memory

This recent story illustrates again how traumatic memory functions.

During a traumatic experience, the amygdalae, those almond-shaped structures deep in your brain that I mentioned briefly in previous chapters, go on red alert. A few of the amygdalae's main jobs are to identify threats to your body's survival and to tag your memories with emotions.

Take my experience with the needle. Long ago, my amygdalae saw that huge needle in my doctor's hands and put a big neon sticky label on it marked, "YOU ALMOST DIED!" Now all I had to do was see a needle like the one from before, and the amygdalae sent my nervous system into hyperdrive. "Danger, Will Robinson! Danger!"

"Phew," the amygdalae were saying to themselves. "We did our job. We warned her." They hadn't had a chance to talk about the needle with the rational frontal lobe because the frontal lobe had left the room when the first experience happened. And the hippocampus was not about to show up for any kind of meeting because it was way too tired. So, the rest of the brain hasn't had a chance to realize how strongly the amygdalae feel about needles like this one and talk some sense to them. My brain as a whole can't recognize that this needle isn't going to cause me to drown the way the previous one had.

The havoc that results from the amygdala's alarm bells seems to them a necessary protection. The brain even goes so far as to recreate aspects of the trauma all over again—in this case, causing me to pee like mad as I had when I took the diuretic, even though I was not having an overload of fluids this time around. (I had only had normal levels of fluids to drink that day, far out of proportion to my urgent need to urinate.)

Traumatically tagged memories like this one can surface with no rational explanation. As you can see from my story, you can even end up feeling like your body has been hijacked. By whom, you know not.

Research has shown that traumatic stress can even physically change the brain. After a highly traumatic event, one like my near drowning, the amygdalae can get stuck in a loop. They keep looking for threats around every corner. They expect, and so find them everywhere. The hippocampus can also become underactive because excessive stress hormones kill off its cells. It should consolidate your memories, helping you understand that the traumatic experience has passed. But in its weakened state, it can't. Instead, your brain keeps signaling that the traumatic situation is still happening. As a result, hormones like cortisol, adrenaline, and norepinephrine remain high, in the long run causing chronic fatigue.

In other words, your sensitivity to the world around you goes through the roof. You become more susceptible to anxiety or panic attacks like the ones I've dealt with for years. Or maybe you simply find yourself overly jumpy and reactive. Exhaustion, the kind that follows you around like a bad hair day, becomes the norm.

To be clear, you don't have to go through a traumatic experience over and over again for it to impact your nervous system significantly. A single instance of overwhelming terror—a threat to your life or safety such as being raped or assaulted, a serious accident or injury, or watching another person be seriously injured or killed—can change your brain's functioning. Not everyone who has an experience like one of these develops Post Traumatic Stress Disorder (PTSD). According to the American Psychiatric Society it is defined as "a psychiatric disorder that may occur in people who have experienced or witnessed a traumatic event, such as a natural disaster, a serious accident, a terrorist act, war/combat, rape or who have been threatened with death, sexual violence, or serious injury." Experiences out of your control do have a higher likelihood of causing it, however. When the trauma occurs repeatedly, chances also go up that it will alter your brain.

The Good News

If all of this sounds depressing, I've got good news, too. Modern brain research has shown us that the brain is highly changeable in positive ways, not just negative ones. Depending on the person's situation it is now possible to heal PTSD with the right tools.

Generally speaking, body-based therapies seem to work best. (Although new research with psychedelics is promising.) Why? Probably because traumatic memory lives outside the realm of language and reason. The frontal lobe (responsible for language and logic) doesn't realize the trauma has happened because it wasn't invited to the party where it all started. In future chapters, I'll share more about NET (mentioned briefly earlier in this chapter) which has supported me tremendously. It's one of many emerging approaches that work in repairing the damage that trauma can leave in its wake.

On the other side of healing comes remembrance. By this I don't mean you remember your past experiences. No, I'm talking about remembering the nature of who you really are. Your oneness with all of life becomes more and more available to you.

That's what I mean when I say you are deathless. You are life itself. Nothing can ever break or harm the real you. And you don't have to die like I did in order to remember it.

CHAPTER 8: WITH NEW EYES

Lesson 8:
*We are never alone.**

Mid-March 2003

Friday. Tonight I've got a date. Possibly (hopefully) a hot one. Paul is taking me to the Honolulu Symphony Orchestra.

I first met Paul David Deering just two weeks after moving to Hawaii in February of 2003. The CDC sent me to Oahu for a work project that lasted from August to December. Like so many others before me, I fell madly in love with the place. For the first time in my life, I made an impulsive decision about my future. I moved to our fiftieth state with no job and no prospects.

"You'll never find a man there," my girlfriends had warned me. "They all live at home because real estate is so expensive, and they are shorter than you." My experiences with Paul so far had not yet disproven them. Paul and I had first bumped into each other at W, a nightclub in Waikiki. Both of us were there only because we had friends looking for dating prospects who had dragged us along. My friend knew Paul and introduced us.

Paul and I swapped contact info. This led to several non-date dates, along the lines of "I'll invite you to some parties and events I'm going to, and you can come along to meet more people since you are new here." Paul made it very clear that he was not at all interested in wining and dining with me, or any other woman for that matter. He had been there, done that. If I did not like him for who he was, then we would part at "Nice to meet you."

But we hit it off after all. And now he has surprised me by asking me on a "real date" (no groups involved). I've been looking forward to

* Source: https://mcusercontent.com/6aeb61681f6c311e999fff730/files/5070a118-63b3-4ac3-87f4-08b4f5d6e2e0/2020_IANDS_Annual_Report.01.pdf pg. 15

attending the orchestra performance with him all week. Finally, the romance I've been wanting!

Except at 3:00 p.m., my abdomen starts cramping. At lightning speed, I am a nine on the pain scale.

Oh shit, I think. Not now, please, not now!

Apparently, the pain doesn't seem nearly as concerned about my upcoming date as I am. It refuses to leave.

Somehow my primary care physician manages to get me in, no small feat for a Friday afternoon. Meekly I don the thin blue gown as I have so many times before. The paper covering the padded table crinkles under me as I wait. Surely the doc will get me out of this fix so I can keep my date.

The news is not good, though. Upon examination, my doctor informs me I need to go to the E.R. for more tests. He suggests I call an ambulance. But surely, I think, once all these tests finish, I can still catch the symphony orchestra? We can go straight from the E.R. to our date, right?

I call Paul. Instead of picking me up at my rental house, can he please come to Straub Clinic in Hawaii Kai? I explain my situation, including the severe pain. Concern in his voice, he answers yes without hesitating.

When he arrives, he finds me doubled over, my face white as a sheet and yelling at some points. Not my best look.

Paul drives us to the Straub Medical Center ER. I notice with some relief, as much as I can feel in this state, that the hospital sits directly across from the Blaisdell Performing Center where the orchestra will be playing in three hours. Fingers crossed; we might still make it.

At check-in they let Paul go with me to the partitioned off "room" where they put me. I am glad for the company at first. Then the nurse gives me the faded blue hospital gown that ties in the back and tells me to change. Everything's off.

I cringe in mortification. Paul will see me, scars and all, in this unforgiving fluorescent light—a far cry from my romantic fantasy of him seeing my body for the first time draped in sexy lingerie. So, I ask him to turn around.

Next comes the intake history. Throughout it I find myself glancing over at Paul. Well, he certainly knows exactly what he'll be getting into if he chooses to ask me out again.

After several tests and at least that many hours, I learned that their first diagnosis of ovarian cysts wasn't accurate so then it was an impacted bowel diagnosis. Given the amount of feces showing up in the colon x-ray they sent me home to empty my bowels from both ends. Scar tissue with a twisted colon from the colostomy I had was the likely cause. At least I won't need surgery, which they were preparing me for until this moment. Paul gave away our two tickets hours ago, knowing we would miss the concert. Eventually I am drugged and discharged.

Paul takes me home. He settles me in with food, *The National Enquirer,* and a "Get Well" balloon. I fall asleep dreaming that this man might turn out to be my knight in shining armor. After all, he didn't leave me.

Making Sense of Love

Throughout my twenties and thirties I struggled in relationships with men. At the time I didn't realize that I kept attracting men like my father: good-looking in a football-player way and emotionally unavailable. I spent all my time trying to please them. At one point early on, I believed I had found a man I thought I could trust to love me, scars and all. Then, after two years, the relationship ended abruptly in betrayal, with him giving me an STD. I felt ashamed, humiliated, and disgusted with myself. For the next fifteen years I chose long-distance relationships and/or being alone to keep myself safe, both physically and mentally. I set unrealistic expectations for what type of man I would date to justify why I wasn't dating. All of this I did without really understanding my own behaviors.

Then in 2000, the lost parts of my memory of the car crash returned. The driver of the car had made an unwanted sexual advance and I said "No." He got angry with me, flooring the gas pedal and jerking the wheel. Before long, the car was crashing into a huge boulder, and I found myself flying through the air toward my death.

Finally, I understood why I could not sustain a relationship. I greatly feared men's anger (hence my need to constantly please them). I had learned that saying "no" to a man could get me killed. This belief system surely had started with my father but relating it to my sexuality was another level. Whether or not I knew this consciously, I lived with it as my emotional reality. No wonder I always worked so hard to please any man I dated. I had been in therapy for years trying to figure this one out and never had. Then, boom, the memory surfaced, and I had complete clarity.

With this shift in awareness, my dating life started to change for the better. I went to a conference in Whistler, Canada, and met a great guy, Ralph. Okay, I was still doing the long-distance thing, and Ralph did look a bit like my father; not everything changes all at once. But I didn't focus on pleasing him or live in mortal terror of his anger. What a great feeling. In the end it didn't last. But it gave me lots of good practice.

Then I made the wild choice to move to Hawaii. After six years at the CDC, I was finding government work unfulfilling, too stifling—possibly another sign of the healing I was experiencing, since before I had felt the security of the job outweighed the annoyances of bureaucracy that came with it. I had checked out New Mexico, but to no avail. I could not fathom living somewhere so brown.

When the CDC sent me to Hawaii on a three-month detail with the Hawaii State Health Department in the fall of 2002, my search ended. The following year I took the leap of moving with no job because I thought that my credentials with the CDC would make finding a position easy. I mean, working for the CDC is the top job for the field of public health - the disease detectives.

Was I in for a shock! No one could have prepared me for how differently things work in the Aloha State. Employers cared not one whit for my fancy resume. I even started to suspect that some people held it against me. I was a haole, the loaded Hawaiian word for a white outsider that literally means "without breath." All too well I understood how it feels to be discriminated against racially.

From the story that opens this chapter, however, you'll see that not everything went badly for me. Against all the odds, and against all the warnings, I had found a man unlike any I had ever known. When our first date ended at the E.R. instead of the Hawaiian Symphony Orchestra, he did not bail. Instead, we got closer. I could be authentic with Paul, vulnerable. Even if my career wasn't flourishing, I had found an excellent reason to stay in the rainbow capital of the world.

In time I also found the courage to buy a house with Paul and move in with him before we were married or even engaged. I mention courage because this choice went against everything my parents had drilled into me. We were living in sin. And they were, of course, appalled. It helped that my brother lived with his partner in sin, so it wasn't just me.

After seventeen months, we married. We are still married today.

More About Paul

When Paul read my first draft of this chapter, his immediate response followed along the lines of, "Hey, this makes me sound like a saint. I sure am not. It took me a lot of years, experiences and mistakes to turn into your loving husband."

His thoughts on the matter had me see the value in sharing a little of his story, too. It further illustrates how the journey toward intimacy can unfold.

Paul pointed out that our two life stories have many parallels. For one thing, we both grew up with at least one narcissistic parent. (Me, I'd say two.) Paul describes his father, John, as intellectually bright but emotionally bankrupt. John knew everyone's weaknesses and used them to undermine and belittle his six children and wife. To deal with it, family members either fought back (to no avail, of course) or cowered in submission. No one survived the ordeal unscathed.

In his first marriage, Paul unconsciously acted out the drama of his childhood. As a kid, he had courageously stood up to his father. While others in the family did their best to stay invisible, Paul frequently argued with John. Then as a husband, Paul became a bully, unwittingly mimicking his father for the seven-year duration of his marriage.

A full fifteen years passed before Paul married again. This time he assumed the victim role. For three years, he let himself be a doormat.

Along the way, though, he was gradually gaining skills for creating healthier relationships. When he began teaching middle school, he quickly realized he needed to understand this volatile, fragile age group better. It led him to pursue an M.Ed. in a program focused on counseling and psychotherapy skills for classroom application. The main body of his coursework involved participating in and learning how to lead encounter group therapy. Paul learned about crucial concepts like "feeling/problem ownership" and the notion that I am responsible for my stuff and you for yours. Along with this, he studied Client-Centered Therapy, developed by Carl Rogers. He then decided that teaching teachers was his calling and went on to get this Ph.D. in Education from the University of Colorado, Boulder.

All this training made Paul a much stronger teacher. It also made him a stronger person. By the time he met me, he had worked out how to be assertive without being abusive, considerate without being a pushover. Because of his past, he also had clear insight into what I had gone through and was continuing to go through with my parents.

Another parallel we have shared revolves around health. In high school, Paul had aimed high. He wanted to attend a top college, where he intended to launch a powerful life of learning and service. He got top grades, too. Because his large family struggled financially, though, he could never hope to achieve his dream without a scholarship.

Luckily, Paul had an ace in the hole. At Cleveland Heights High, he had emerged as a star football player. More than one school had sent letters of interest, offering him potential scholarships that could put him where he wanted to be.

Then Paul's luck ran out. One Friday night, the day before he and his father would be taking a trip to the University of Pittsburgh to meet with football coaches, Paul broke his leg at the knee during his football game. In an instant, his football and track careers ended. With them, his scholarships also vanished as he did not understand the system of academic scholarships, only sports.

Ultimately Paul attended Cleveland State University. Living a hand-to-mouth existence in a cold, rundown inner-city apartment, Paul supported himself through school. He got a solid education, though it certainly hadn't come easily.

In terms of our life together, this experience has had everything to do with Paul's compassionate response to my own health obstacles.

Bottom line: By the time I met Paul at the W on that fateful evening, he was ready for me. He has been able to ride with me through the tumultuous waves of health trials and emotional upsets without ever seeking to abandon ship.

No one with family histories like ours could realistically expect to know, without effort, how to create a healthy relationship. But anyone can change her or his trajectory. Dealing with your past prepares you to find Mr. or Mrs. Right. By this I don't mean you'll find a perfect person, but rather someone who is a perfect fit for you, the way that Paul fits me.

At the time of this writing, Paul and I have been together for eighteen joyful, if challenging, years. And life just keeps getting better for us.

New Eyes

With the stability of my relationship with Paul came a growing ability to reframe the events of my life. We all know the adage about hindsight. I'm not talking about looking back on my life with regrets about my mistakes, though. I was discovering the ability to see them with more love and understanding than ever.

For one thing, Paul helped me see things his way. Instead of judging my body for all the things it could not do, like I did so often, Paul kept pointing out the many things it could do, in spite of all it had endured. I had not failed in my life, he insisted when I went down that road of self-criticism. Instead, he always reminded me, I had come through so much, so well. He even put the picture of the crashed, crumpled convertible in a picture frame to help me remember what an incredible thing I had survived.

Beyond anything he said, Paul's loving presence in my life caused me to rethink so many of my earlier assumptions. Doctors had sewed me up after the accident, but that didn't mean I was okay. How desperately I had insisted on getting plastic surgeries back in my twenties. I had several of them to help minimize scarring on my thighs and face. I tried liposuction on my left thigh hoping it would "firm up" the major muscle atrophy that had occurred there. It didn't. At one point I even went so far as to get breast implants (which I had removed a decade or so later after I was told one ruptured- turns out it had not).

At the time of these many procedures, my mom thought I was nuts for adding unnecessary surgeries that would put my life at risk, given what I had lived through already. She couldn't understand that my self-esteem was tanking. I felt so self-conscious about the scars that I learned to sit with my legs crossed at the ankles to hide the skin graft on my left one. I slathered on gallons of Vitamin E, hoping it would cause the scars to fade. It helped, but only a little. So, I always dressed in clothes that would cover the scars so people wouldn't ask what had happened. Surely with all this disfigurement, I would never find love.

Yet now, on the other side of a big wave of healing, love had found me. The first healthy relationship I had ever experienced came from showing, not hiding, my wounds. I had spent years trying to make my body more desirable to men, only to discover I was actually just trying to make it desirable to myself. No amount of outside effort could accomplish that, though. Only I could deem myself worthy as-is. Paul's support helped me to do this.

The more I aligned myself with Paul's version of me, the more I found myself aligned with new versions of other parts of my life, too. I began to see the car accident as not an accident. I don't mean my parents' take on the story, either. I had not gotten scorched as punishment by God the day it happened. Rather, my own Soul had its reasons for allowing this event to unfold.

When I looked back on it, I saw how totally unsuited I had been for military service. I am not judging it as wrong for other people, and I understand the role that the military plays in our world. But now I understand that a life in the Air Force would have killed me. Shoot—I can't even stand small planes. I get claustrophobic in them. Yet back in school, I couldn't grasp any of this. I had placed my father's wishes and my need for his approval above all else. Definitely I would have kept on at the Academy until my last breath if not for the car crash. After that, I would have continued pleasing my father with a military career, one which would have made me miserable. I even had to admit to myself that I had secretly hoped, back in the ICU, that I would not recover from the accident enough to return to the Academy. My father wanted this for me above all else at the time. I would rather have stayed ill than go back. Of course, the reality was, based on the extent of my injuries, I was never going back. I became a disabled veteran (DV) and still am.

Then I had tried to make up for my failure to graduate from the AFA by having an important career. Maybe my father didn't care so much for what I was doing. Still, he couldn't deny I had achieved something. I worked for the CDC, no easy job to pull down. I owned my own home, a nice one, and provided for myself completely. See, Dad. I'm somebody.

But in Hawaii, I no longer had a fancy career. Heck, I felt lucky just to find a job that fit my training as a project manager at the University of Hawaii School of Public Health. No longer could I use my achievements to prop myself up or prove something to my absent, yet ever-present, father. Finally, I had a great relationship at age thirty-nine, yes, but one which my father did not approve of because Paul had been divorced (twice) and Paul stood up to him, whether it was politics, religion, or me. He had only agreed to meet my husband at my wedding, where he made his displeasure painfully clear to all.

In other words, I was facing new questions of identity. I had carried around inside myself certain ideas. Your job needs to be like this. Your house needs to look like this. Your relationship needs to go like this. In all those cases, the "this" referred to the expectations of my family and their world, along with the larger American culture. Here in Hawaii, nothing I did or had looked like "this" anymore. I had lived in sin with my husband Paul. Then even as a married unit, we hardly fit the mainstream ideal. The cost of living forced us to stay on a budget, which didn't include a large house or fancy cars. According to the cost-of-living index for 2022, Hawaii is the most expensive state to live in. As of 2021, Google says to live "comfortably" in Hawaii you need to be making an annual salary of $122,000. With minimum wage being $10.10 per hour that is unrealistic for most people. My work as an independent registered dietitian, while respectable and in my field, could hardly qualify as career-making.

All of it was forcing me to rethink and redefine success on my own terms.

In reflecting on all of this, I could now see that the accident had the hand of my Higher Self in it. It had broken me free. Free from a career I could never enjoy. Free from the oppressive religion of my parents. Free from a culture that needed to keep me in an extremely narrow box.

In other words, the accident broke me free from the bonds of a small life. Before it happened, I had received so much praise for being a people pleaser. No other scenario I can come up with, unless fairly life-altering like the crash had been, could have broken me loose from that pattern. No, it didn't break me loose magically, the day I flew from the car. But it put me on the road to freeing myself. Dealing with the aftermath of that fateful day forced me to actively pursue growth and healing in my life, again and again. As a good Kerr girl, I never would have done this. Even with its many challenges, this car accident has brought so many gifts from my soul.

I like to think that I actually did graduate from the Academy. Not with a degree, of course. Rather, my Higher Self decided I had graduated from a way of being and doing things that the Academy symbolized. The time had come for me to move beyond it. At the car crash, I matriculated into coursework that would take me into a whole new way of life.

Fifteen Prop and Wings

For more than three decades after the car crash, I carried around the idea that I had been a terrible cadet. After high grades in high school, I found myself struggling to scrape by with a C average at the A.F.A. I had zero interest in engineering, a major focus of my coursework. As I've shared, I also found myself at the back of the pack when it came to any of the Academy's physical activities, like running or target practice. The place had not lost out when it lost me, I always told myself.

That is, until recently, when I stumbled across my Prop and Wings pins.

At the end of every fourth-class (freshman) year at the Academy, cadets get to experience recognition. This three-day Hell Week finale of the year acknowledges that the fourth-class cadets have now joined the ranks of the upperclassmen and can wear the Prop and Wings insignia on their flight caps. Cadets in the years above can use their own money during this time to buy Prop and Wings pins, which they can give to any fourth-class cadets they want to personally acknowledge.

What a surprise I got when I reflected on the fact that I had received fifteen of them, more than anyone else in my squadron. So many upperclassmen had taken the time to acknowledge me for how much I had improved.

Was I the best cadet in the class? Not by a long stretch. But maybe I hadn't been the worst, either. I'm not saying the sight of the pins changed my mind about my not being cut out for the Air Force. It did feel good, though, to look at things with new eyes. My courage and determination had shone through, even back then. I just couldn't see it yet myself.

October 2020

By now, the country has grappled with the horror of the COVID-19 pandemic for almost a year. Night after night I have watched numbers rise and fall. The number of cases, rising. The number of beds falling. The number of available ventilators, plummeting. The number of our dead, up, up, so much further up. Long ago, the U.S. pandemic eclipsed the 9-11 death rate of 2,996. We now measure deaths with those kinds of numbers on a daily basis—deaths no one will honor with funerals.

It has taken a toll on all of us.

And it has taken me into the territory of introspection. Perhaps because of my past, I find myself ruminating on the nature of death itself.

On any given night, I see images of nurses, doctors, and other healthcare professionals, covered head to toe in personal protective equipment. For many, these alien-looking workers will be the last people they see before they cross to the other side. So often I hear this cited as one of the biggest horrors that the pandemic brings, the prospect of facing death without loved ones near.

The concept of dying alone terrifies most of us. Psychic medium Julie Ryan often receives the question from her clients, "Did my loved one die alone?" Her response, "You are absolutely right in believing your parents were surrounded by angels and the spirits of deceased loved ones and pets as they transitioned. In fact, no one dies alone. "

That's what Julie discusses in her book *Angelic Attendants: What Really Happens As We Transition From This Life Into The Next* and it's validated and corroborated by many healthcare, hospice, and funeral professionals. In addition, Christopher Kerr, MD, found close to 90% of end-of-life patients report seeing the spirits of deceased loved ones and pets in *Death Is But A Dream*."

Think of how many people you know or have heard of who waited until their loved ones left the room to make their transition to the other side. My own brother-in-law, who suffered from amyotrophic lateral sclerosis (ALS), found himself in a house packed with people who loved him as his death neared. Yet he chose to go when no one was around him. Same with my mother-in-law, Regina.

With that in mind, I would like to respectfully challenge your fears about dying alone. The human mind, the human eyes, look at a situation when others are not nearby and say, "I'm here alone." But what if we reframe this?

You cannot be alone. It's impossible. Guides, angels, and beings of love and light surround you at all times. Many loving humans also wish to support you, whether or not you realize it. If you feel alone, you are simply feeling disconnected—in your awareness only, not in reality—from the Source of love inside yourself.

Maybe it seems strange for me to bring this up in a chapter I've devoted to the joy of finding my life partner, Paul. But somehow, I can't tell that story without also sharing what this experience, as well as my time out of the body, has taught me about loneliness. For nineteen years of my life, I lived alone. No roommates, no pets. Beyond a few houseplants, I had no one to share my life with from day to day. I know well the pain of loneliness. I could even say I became a living radio beacon broadcasting the repeating message, "I am alone! I am alone!"

Yet I can tell you clearly, those feelings of loneliness were something I created. I never really was alone. I had so much love and support around me all the time. But I kept myself so busy putting out that message "I'm alone!" that I couldn't receive all the love trying to reach me.

My relationship, when it came, did not actually cure me of loneliness. If a relationship really can do that, then why do so many of us feel so alone while inside of relationships? I certainly had in my relationships with my family of origin, as well as in many of the romantic relationships I pursued. I won't deny that my relationship with Paul brought emotional support. Paul is such a supportive person that naturally it would. But the truth of the matter? I used this relationship as my excuse to let love in. Paul's many loving messages helped me amplify the burgeoning self-love I was already beginning to discover when we met.

That self-love is how I finally overcame the many years of loneliness—which I now understand was actually a feeling of disconnection, not from other people, but from myself.

When my mother got the call about my accident, she received hardly any details about what had happened to me. She just knew "things were bad." She had received the message about my accident in the middle of the night and could not get on a plane until the next day. As she traveled across the country, her mind invented a hundred terrifying storylines. Most prominently, she worried I would die alone.

But I already had. At the accident, the driver of the car that threw me was still fully conscious, even after the crash. Yet never once did he come over to see if I was okay. By the time caring people showed up, I had already left my body for the other side.

And there, beyond my body, I was the opposite of alone. Angels surrounded me. Love enveloped me. The love was me, and I was it. This I/we was one with everything and everyone. In that state, I could not have conjured the word "alone," even if I had tried. Thinking about it makes me understand why some Indigenous cultures mourn at a baby's birth and rejoice at an elder's death. Here on earth, we face the greatest challenge of feeling separated from God. My experience has taught me that loneliness itself is a lie, or at least based on one.

I understand fully why people want their loved ones to have physical contact at the time of death. But I believe they want it for themselves more than for the person who is transitioning. They might do well to ask themselves, "Is this actually me trying to make peace with my own mortality and feelings of disconnection?"

We've all heard the old saying, you come into this world alone, and you will leave it alone one day. I think you could more accurately put it, you come into this world with nothing, materially speaking, and you will leave with nothing. But never once are you alone or judged.

Think about it. During nearly all births, a doctor or midwife guides and supports a baby into the world. Even if you did not have one of these, you did have at the very least, your mother. Once someone cut your umbilical cord, the person probably put you on her chest.

Now think about death. When you die, guides will meet you, just as they did me. Like midwives, they will support you through your birth into the new world you have entered. On that side, you will know clearly...

You are not and have never been alone.

CHAPTER 9: CALLING ALL ANGELS

Lesson 9: *Remember to ask the Angels for help.*

Fall 2008

As we pass through Monument, Colorado, I notice my heart rate increasing. The crash happened here.

Soon we see the signs for the Air Force Academy North and South Gate entrances. How many times I went in and out of those gates as a cadet, usually only grateful upon exiting. I never made it back in through the North Gate on Sunday, August 28, 1983.

Now I'm here again. Paul has taken me along for a business meeting in Denver. When he had asked me, in Hawaii, if I would be interested in joining him and perhaps going back to Colorado Springs, the thought came, "For what?" But then I started thinking how it might feel to meet some of my medical team from the time of the accident, this time healthy and standing upright. I heard this little voice inside me say, "Go and see them." Over the years I have learned that when I hear that voice I need to listen. Call it intuition, Spirit, God—whatever the name, when I do not follow its guidance, I usually regret it.

Yesterday, after a long red-eye flight and a few short hours at the hotel, I met with Nurse Sandy Haugen and her husband, Tug, followed by dinner with paramedic John Hartling and his wife, Karen. This morning we sat down with Dr. Amilu Stewart and her husband, Bill Perry, and now we're visiting the scene of the accident.

More than a quarter of a century has passed since the crash. Yet I find myself reliving so many memories from that time, most of them not so great. I had prepared myself for that. What I hadn't expected, though? My medical team from back then still has vivid memories, too, of the time they spent caring for me.

EMT, John Hartling

John, a Navy veteran, describes himself as your classic Type A personality. He became an Emergency Medical Technician (EMT) because his new job kept him busy for only forty hours a week, nothing compared to his usual sixty. To fill the extra time, he started volunteering with the local fire department and became a first responder.

John has won the Phoenix Award three times in his career as an EMT. The State of Colorado gives the award to a healthcare provider for bringing someone thought to be clinically dead back to life. One of those times was my case. John has performed CPR about five times in his career, pretty unusual considering that some never administer it once throughout their whole time of service.

When I ask John about the scariest moment for him in my case, he instantly replies.

> *"When I arrived at the scene, people told me you were already dead. They had you covered up with a blanket and told me I should go work with the other person (as we did not know you were cadets from the AFA.) I decided to make my own decision. Then I could get no sign of life from you. As a last resort, I gave you a sternal rub. It's a very painful way to get a response. When your eyelid flickered and pupil dilated, I decided to work with you. At that point, I was scared to death that you were alive, and I would not be able to keep you alive!"*

In our conversation, John explains that CPR typically has long odds. Despite the statistics they tell you in the classes, only 1-2% of people who receive it come back. "You were one of them," he tells me somberly. Even CDC says "currently, about 9 in 10 people who have cardiac arrest outside the hospital die. But CPR can help improve those odds. If it is performed in the first few minutes of cardiac arrest, CPR can double or triple a person's chance of survival.

Many weeks after John had dropped me off at the ER, he came back to see me. He did this not as part of his medical duties, but rather from a personal commitment. Because he knows from experience how it feels to sit in the hospital with no visitors, he goes out of his way to call on people there, including people he has never met.

John's three documented saves speak volumes. Without him, I would have died.

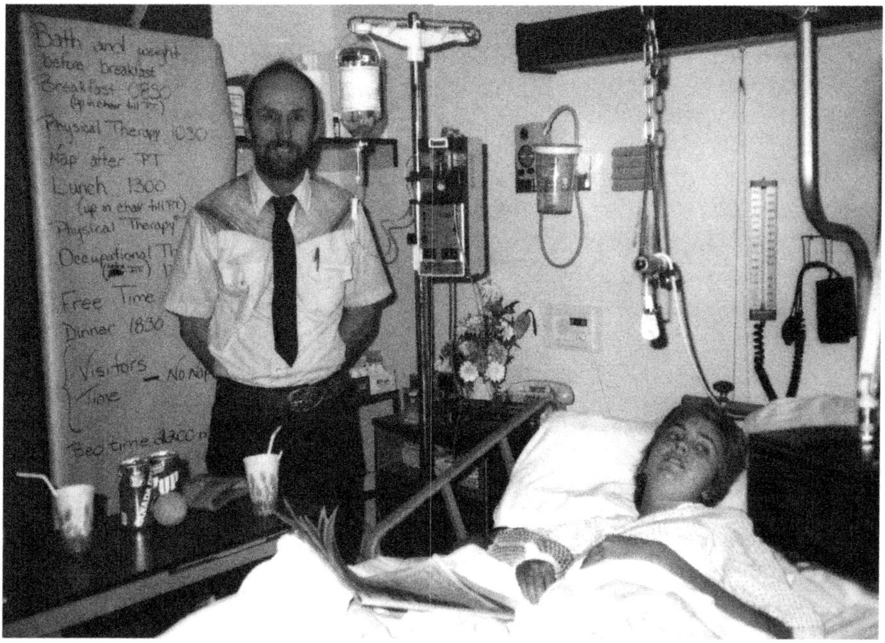

EMT John Hartling visited me in the hospital approximately ten weeks after the crash. I was speechless that he would do such a kind thing. He filled in some of the blanks in my story, from when he arrived to dropping me off at Penrose Community Hospital. I did not remember any of it.

Surgeon, Dr. Amilu Stewart, M.D.

When Paul and I met with Dr. Amilu Stewart, I was tickled to learn that my surgeon was a pioneer, a true maverick. Back in the early 1960s, when Dr. Stewart went to medical school, the thought of a woman doctor made people laugh. This didn't stop her, though. She graduated with the first female class at Jefferson Medical College in Philadelphia. Then she went on to become the first female surgeon in Colorado Springs as well as the first female president of the Western Surgical Association.

When Dr. Stewart got the emergency call for my accident, she had been practicing for eleven years. I have since learned how rare it was, a fluke, really, for a surgeon with such experience and expertise to be on call for a case like mine.

Now, twenty-five years later and thirty-six years into her career as a surgeon, Dr. Stewart still vividly remembers my case. Here's a paraphrased version of her first moments with me, written from her voice.

The time you must exchange information in an emergency situation is minimal, seconds, maybe a minute or two. I had my first moments with Nicole in the hall, heading into the OR. In a few sentences, the EMT explained events at the scene of the accident—a young woman thrown out of a car, covered with a blanket by the time he arrived and assumed dead. His assessment: the woman was unconscious with a very weak pulse prompting him to start resuscitation.

Now I could see for myself that this young woman was bleeding from the bone, a medical phenomenon that occurs during extreme shock. The body's circulation bypasses extremities, diverting as much blood as possible to vital organs, the heart and brain. I didn't even know this woman's name yet since she had no identification on her. What I did know, though, was that the teenage girl in my hands hovered very close to death.

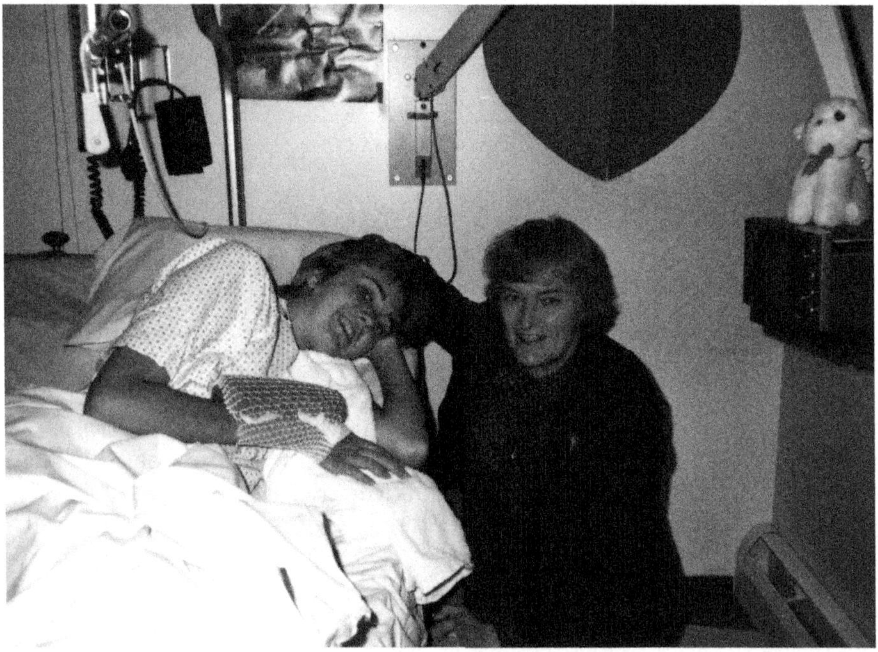

Dr. Stewart and me during her daily rounds at Penrose Community Hospital, Oct. 1983.

During my extended stay in the ICU Dr. Stewart performed multiple surgeries on me. Now she reminds me that I went through several "near-death" experiences in the hospital, such as the time my heart stopped while they were moving me from my hospital bed onto the stretcher to go to the operating room. They had to resuscitate me on the stretcher just to get me to the operating room. During that surgery my body was so unstable they could only give me limited anesthesia and a muscle relaxant. With too many drugs, she knew they would lose me. So I could hear voices and feel pulling at my abdomen yet could not move. And then there was the fluid overload in my lungs where I felt like I was drowning, a diuretic given as a last option saved me.

Hearing Dr. Stewart's stories from that time does something to me. I'm moved to connect with this woman who has irrevocably changed my life through a devotion to her calling as a surgeon. Considering the level of skill, stamina, and compassion my case called for, I know our paths did not cross accidentally.

Registered Nurse, Sandy Haugan

Sandy, a tall, lean cowgirl, had served as an ICU/pediatric nurse for 10 years when she met me shortly after I entered the hospital. Her story of becoming a nurse bears the mark of synchronicity that she describes as "a God thing." She had always planned to become an airline stewardess, but then she got too tall for the job. Out of money and out of plans, she put herself on a waiting list for nursing school. With at least one hundred people in line ahead of her, she suspected this plan would turn out like the others, in the slush pile. Still, she would try, even though it might take years before anything came of it. To that end, she found herself standing at the door of the admissions office one afternoon when the manager of the program received an unexpected call. One of their new students had gone to the hospital with phenylketonuria and would not be able to start school yet. As he hung up the phone, he looked up to see Sandy standing there. "Do you want to be a nurse?" he asked? She answered enthusiastically, "Yes!"

Thirty-five years later, and twenty-five years after she cared for me, Sandy can recall my case in detail:

"The scariest moment for me was seeing you in the ICU when you had just coded. Your abdomen was packed with dressings and left wide open. You ran a temperature over 104 degrees, and your hair was wet from the sweat of the fever. Your eyes... you had giant, wild eyes. Obviously, you felt frightened and out of control. You hardly had any clothes on. People were not paying attention to your privacy, the kind of thing that would matter to a nineteen-year-old girl.

"Your case was very critical. In the beginning stages, we were still making sure you would not expire. The accident was so severe and traumatic that we constantly worried you would throw a blood clot, a fat clot out of your broken bones, or develop septicemia. Those three things were your enemy. You were so critical it required a couple of nurses to take care of you, nurses we had to bring in from the main hospital.

"Another crucial piece of your care was determining how well your brain was working. I was always asking you, 'Do you know what time it is?' Or 'Do you know your mom? Do you recognize people?' I tried to inject humor, but it didn't always go over well.

"Dr. Stewart would check on you twice a day, morning, and night. Then we would call in any changes to your orders. We had you on multiple antibiotics, multiple IV lines. You would beg us not to turn you over, which we had to do to prevent bed sores, and you'd plead with us not to change your many dressings. Everything caused you severe pain.

"When they finally moved you to the pediatric wing after seven weeks in ICU, they put you in a room in the far corner with a bleak view. Other than a little sun from the East in the morning, your room didn't have much to engage you with the outside world. So, your nursing team had to engage you. You wouldn't watch television, couldn't read, couldn't write. You didn't really seem to enjoy anything. So much of your care was painful and uncomfortable.

"One of your turning points came when you got a colostomy. Of course, you were very upset about having this procedure done. But I sure was grateful. At least that midline incision that had been clamped with rubber hoses was finally closed shut. No matter how much you hated it, I knew this was moving you forward.

"Some of the nurses thought your case was too much work. It required a high level of detail, and your mom was always there watching. Being watched makes some people uncomfortable about doing this kind of work. Not me. I always saw your mom as part of my team. My philosophy has always been that family members are part of my team. When it came time to move you out of the ICU, your mom and I successfully petitioned to get you moved to pediatrics, my home base.

"During her evening visits, your mom and I would rub your toes. You had major nerve damage on your right foot that caused immense pain. We would fix your hair, scratch your back, put clean sheets under you. We would try to cool your skin off by turning the fans on around you and tuck you in for what we hoped would be a good night's sleep. Those little details bonded us. I honestly liked doing all of this for you.

"Being the oldest of six children, and the only girl, I had developed some personality quirks along the way, including being an 'order person.' It came in handy in taking care of you. I worked hard to keep your room in order. I opened the cartons on your tray, opened your napkin for you. I know it sounds like nothing, taking care of minute details like these. But I knew they were really important. These things were all there was to your existence at that time.

"All four of my children know about you, Nicole. Over the years, I have shared your miraculous story with them and others. I told my kids that the person driving the car you rode in had been drinking. All my children understand that even if they make bad decisions, they can still call home to ask me for a ride.

"You are the only patient I have kept in touch with this long. You were a joy for me."

When we arrive for our dinner with Sandy, she is already there and rearranging the table settings, just so. You could easily fault her for this. Yet the incredible attention to detail that came so naturally to her meant everything in my case. Sandy had given a tremendous amount of concentrated care to me in a way I genuinely needed. When other nurses threw up their hands with me, Sandy swooped in. She scooped me up and watched over me like her own.

I feel so grateful that Nurse Sandy came into my life when I needed her most. More than anyone else on my team, my family and I got to know and love her. She served in the trenches for me, without complaint.

I share Sandy's comments about the colostomy with you because this part of my story has an interesting twist. The news of the colostomy surgery had hit me hard. Like Nurse Sandy, Dr. Stewart said that the procedure had saved my life; without it, they never could have contained the many infections that continued to threaten me. But I, at age nineteen, could not fathom a life of dealing with its side-effects. Bag changes, unpredictable discharges of feces, unpleasant odors, wearing clothes with elastic waistbands—not to mention how all that would affect my sex life. Would I ever be normal again?

I still had not really made peace with this surgery on the eve of yet another one, this time to remove my gallbladder. My medical team hoped it would be the last major procedure I would have to undergo. My gallbladder had formed massive gallstones during my stay in the ICU because of the many intense medications it had to process. I had already tried to deal with the stones through a low-fat diet, which I had followed strictly – for the most part. I confess that Mom did bring in pizza one night, hoping I would finally eat something. Over the course of the months in the hospital on the diet, I had dropped twenty-five pounds that my body could not afford to lose. I had hoped the pizza could somehow keep me from needing the surgery. But I took one bite and vomited it right back up.

We had to take more serious measures.

When I met Dr. Stewart for the pre-surgery appointment, I told her I had been praying very hard for God to dissolve the gallstones. I truly believed they could and would dissolve on their own through divine intervention.

"Nicole, do you want the good news or the bad news?" Dr. Stewart asked.

My heart sank.

"Go ahead and give me the bad news first." By now I had trained myself to get the bad stuff out of the way.

Tears swelled in my eyes as Dr. Stewart explained that the stones had not dissolved. Indeed, I would still need the surgery. Both God and my body had let me down.

"Well," I said limply, "then what's the good news?"

"It seems the cut between your anal and sphincter muscle has healed. I will be able to reverse your colostomy in the same operation."

I sat stunned. A stern Polish woman named Frieta, my colostomy nurse, had already left me a pamphlet on living with the challenges of an "-ostomy." She and others had led me to believe that the procedure to divert my stools was permanent. I had prayed so hard, for so long, to have the gallstones dissolve that I could not see the possibility of even greater things happening.

At that moment, though, as Dr. Stewart explained more on reversing the colostomy, I understood. Even if I didn't get the answers I hoped for, God always heard my prayers.

I have been living without my gallbladder now for over thirty-eight years, with minimal side effects. I think about it a lot. When I am set in my expectations of how I want things to turn out, I remind myself of this experience. Nicole, I tell myself, trust that God knows the bigger picture. Take a step back and see with God's eyes.

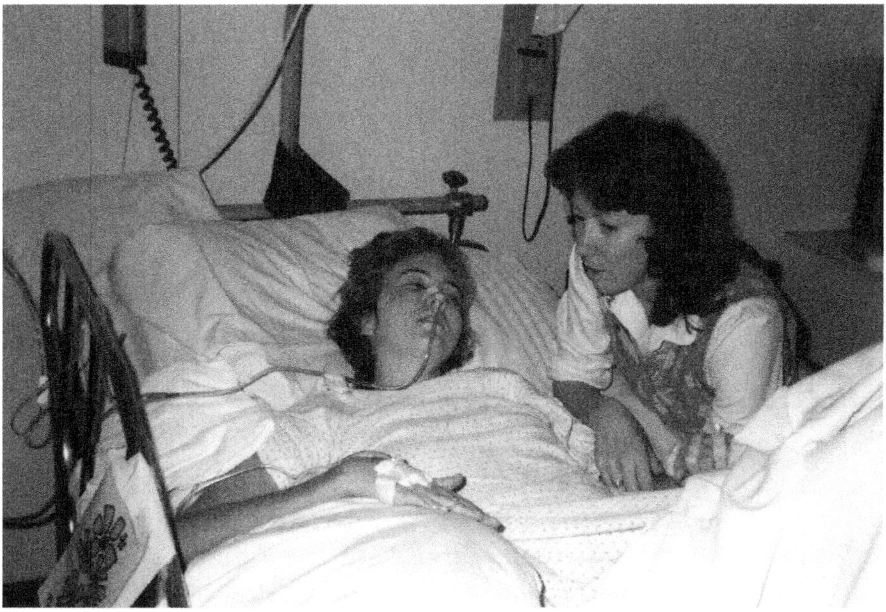

Nurse Sandy's attentiveness and attention to detail shown here.

My Cadet Sponsor, Captain Jan Williamson

Even though Paul and I did not visit her that weekend in Colorado Springs, I cannot tell the story of the people who supported me through the accident without sharing the story of Captain Jan Williamson.

As a freshman (fourth degree), I had been assigned Jan as my sponsor. The sponsor program gave us cadets a home away from home, a place on weekends where we could do things like sleep until noon, wash laundry, and eat a home-cooked meal.

Single, smart, fun, and, I thought, very hip, Jan provided a haven for me. She had two cats, Jock and Strap, who could entertain us for hours. Most importantly, she understood the many challenges of being a female in the military. Her care and generosity always put me at ease after a tough week (which was pretty much all of them). Jan's home became my one escape, a link to the "real" world outside of the Academy.

Here's how she describes what she experienced on August 29:

"Monday was a normal morning at work for me in the Academy Registrar's office until I heard co-workers talking about a terrible car accident involving a couple of cadets. The girl cadet had been seriously injured. Somehow, I knew it was you, even before I confirmed it. Don't ask me how. I called your squadron, Tiger Ten, and found out you had been taken to Penrose Community Hospital. I rushed down there, not knowing what I would find.

"When I arrived, somehow, I was allowed into your ICU room. I guess they thought I was "in loco parentis" as your sponsor. Had they not told me it was you, Nicole, I would never, ever have been able to I.D. you. Your entire body, especially your face, was so badly swollen, battered and bruised. You were unrecognizable.

"You gave us a lot of scary moments. The one that stands out most for me was the night you had emergency surgery. That night we kept vigil, having learned that you might not make it. Two of my dear friends kept me company in the waiting room as we took turns sitting by your bedside. It was the middle of the night, and the lights were very dim in the intensive care room. I dozed off for a moment, but I remember looking over at you. You were on a ventilator and couldn't speak, but I'll never forget that look in your eyes. You wore such a look of desperation. I felt like you were pleading with me to help you, to remove the tube. In that surgery they cut you wide open. I will never forget seeing your abdomen packed open."

For the first couple of months of my hospital stay, my mom slept at Jan's house, in the same room I had used for my weekend escapes. When Jan changed jobs and no longer worked at the Academy, she still came to visit me on her way home. After a trip to Korea, she came back to tell me the story of the fantastic man she had just met, the one she would eventually marry. How good it felt to have a friend during that dark time, one who could tell me girl stuff and laugh with me.

In fact, Jan and I have remained friends ever since. In 2004, she attended my wedding as one of my flower ladies. Memories had flooded her at that event of how no one had known, at the time of my accident, if I would survive or ever walk again, never mind walk down the aisle.

In her notes to me, she wrote, "Your accident and the circumstances of your rescue and recovery changed me forever. You went through a lot, physically, emotionally, and psychologically. So did the rest of us. And, if ever I saw the power of prayer, it was during this time."

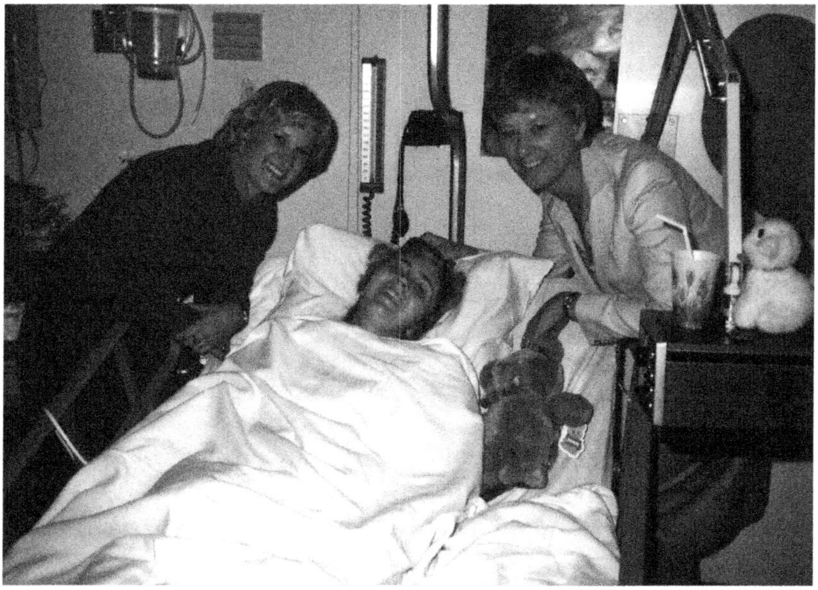

Captain Jan and Cadet Tina stopping by to try and lift my Spirit.

My Mom, Erika S. Kerr

As I reflected on these people who supported me, I realized that I had to acknowledge my mother for all she did during a terribly harrowing time.

Due to the communication complications that existed in the age before cell phones, Mom didn't hear about the accident immediately. She relates:

> *"On Monday, August 29, I got the call that every parent dreads. The call that makes your heart stop, changes your life forever and gives you nightmares for years to come. Just like in the movies, it came in the middle of the night."*

Mom had received this horrible news from a neighbor around 1:00 am CST after having done a round-trip drive from our home in Jackson to New Orleans airport. My parents had dropped my little brother, Sean, off at the airport so he could start his first (and only) year at the Marine Military Academy. As soon as they could identify me, The AFA started trying to reach my parents. After hours of trying, they were finally able to reach my sister Rachel in Dallas to let her know they needed to get in touch with our parents. Rachel, having no idea where our parents were, called our dear neighbor, Mrs. Carolyn Burns, and told her the situation. "Nicole was in an accident and is in the hospital." Mrs. Burns, to her credit, kept calling Mom until she finally reached her a little after 1:00 am. She relayed what little she knew. Until the offices of the AFA opened, all Mom could do was wait.

Finally, the sun came up and 8:00 a.m. arrived. I had been lying in bed, sleepless, just watching the clock tick. Those were the longest seven hours of my life.

When Mom finally got through, the captain on my squadron began with, "Mrs. Kerr, Nicole was in a bad car accident and is in the hospital. We are not authorized to tell you whether or not you should come. However, if you do decide to come, I will pick you up at the airport and take you to see her."

All through that day and through most of the next one, my mom waited. When she finally got off of the plane in Colorado and stepped into my captain's waiting car, worries still plagued her.

What had happened? Why had God sent this trial? Was I still alive?

Then the waiting ended.

"I took one look at my daughter and bit my lip so I wouldn't cry. Nicole was alive, but barely.

"My daughter was so swollen I hardly recognized her. Her skin was grayish, almost rubbery. They had her hooked up to every tube you can imagine. I had only seen something like this in the movies. I counted: One, two, three... up to ten IV bags hanging from sterile poles, all leading into her fragile veins. Her beautiful, blonde hair was filthy. Grit, gravel and pebbles still remained embedded in her scalp. A big abrasion across the right side of her face showed exposed, red, raw flesh.

"In the background, I heard the nurse giving the rundown of Nicole's injuries. Broken pelvis, broken wrist, broken ankle,

partially amputated foot, multiple infections... and more. I could not comprehend that the nurse was saying all those horrible things about my child.

"After a few moments, Nicole opened her big blue eyes.

" 'Mom, how long are you going to stay?' she asked me.

"I leaned over, giving her a gentle kiss on the non-burned side of her face.

" 'As long as necessary.'

"With that, I stepped out of her room. In the hallway, I broke into tears."

Not until the day after she arrived would Mom finally get to meet with Dr. Stewart, the first person to give Mom concrete answers about my condition.

"Dr. Stewart used words like sepsis, gangrene, hypovolemic shock. I had no idea what any of those words meant; but they all sounded bad. The doctor kept reiterating that Nicole was full of fiberglass and other toxic debris that was causing multiple infections, hence the high fever. They were desperately trying to avoid taking her into surgery again and cutting her open. She reported Nicole had lost a lot of blood and her vital signs were not looking good.

"She ended by saying, 'Nicole is a very, very, very sick girl.'

"Well, I finally had the prognosis. Really, really, really bad news."

The "as long as necessary" promise Mom had made to me turned out to require four months of her life to fulfill. She slept at Jan's house, emphasizing the word "slept," because all her waking hours she spent at the hospital. To sustain herself, Mom started every day with a cup of hot tea and a Twinkie. Then she climbed into the borrowed truck of Jan's good friend, Captain Ruthie, to make the twenty-minute drive to the hospital.

"As I got closer to the hospital, fear would set in. I would think, will a nurse or doctor greet me today with the news that Nicole has passed away?

"Just like the doctors, I had my rounds to make when I arrived. I would go immediately to check on Nicole. I always seemed to find a nurse tending to her. No surprise. Nicole's care was very high maintenance, with bandages to change and IV bags to switch out all the time. It took two busy nurses to cover it all.

"When Dr. Stewart came in, I would always ask, 'How is she doing?' After a while, I started to get used to one of her three replies: Either, 'No change, still the same,' or, 'A bit better,' or my least favorite one, 'A lot worse.'

During that time, my mom spent twelve hours a day, seven days a week, at that hospital. For lunch or dinner, she would grab a quick meal in the cafeteria, usually just a bowl of soup. While I slept, she often found herself leading a group of my friends, which she called my "fan club," in rounds of prayer at my bedside. She also enlisted more than 5,000 people worldwide to pray for me. When not caring for me, Mom began to make rounds to other patients in my hall, bringing them hot chocolate and all the treats my friends had given me that I could not eat. She also played Mama Bear for me, especially when officials moved me to the military hospital. Each and every day, Mom stayed until visiting hours ended at 10:00 p.m.

Mom witnessed so many ups and downs during my hospital stay. At one point, my doctor even told her, "Erika, it's out of my hands," and pointed towards the ceiling, indicating God would make the call about whether or not I would live. Mom sat through so many hours of uncertain surgeries and treatments with unknown outcomes. She almost watched me die the day my lungs filled with fluid multiple times, an event I have described in an earlier chapter.

"Witnessing Nicole's recovery was like riding a rollercoaster. I arrived one morning to find a notice on her door about blood transfusions. I walked in to find Dr. Stewart and several nurses working on Nicole. I thought, 'Lord, what is happening now?' It turns out they had given Nicole three pints of blood, and all of it went straight through her into her colostomy bag.

"Nicole did not seem upset about it, though. At this point in her care, she had developed an attitude of, 'Whatever happens, happens.' She seemed to cope with things better than me."

The thought of being operated on by Air Force Academy doctors had terrified me. My mom knew that. When military doctors, not my trusted Dr. Stewart, started talking about performing another surgery, Mom accomplished the impossible. She found a way to have me readmitted to Penrose, where Dr. Stewart worked. This meant my parents had to take financial responsibility for the rest of my care, which included a $7,000 re-admittance fee just for starters. Mom did this without flinching.

Finally, when Mom succeeded in getting me to eat six French fries and half a small hamburger, she rejoiced. Soon we would go home.

When I reflect on what my mother did for me during this time, I truly feel a sense of inexpressible gratitude. Perhaps some people think she only did her duty, a "mother's job." Probably Mom thinks of it this way herself. Still, I've been around long enough now to know that plenty of mothers could never have shown up the way she did.

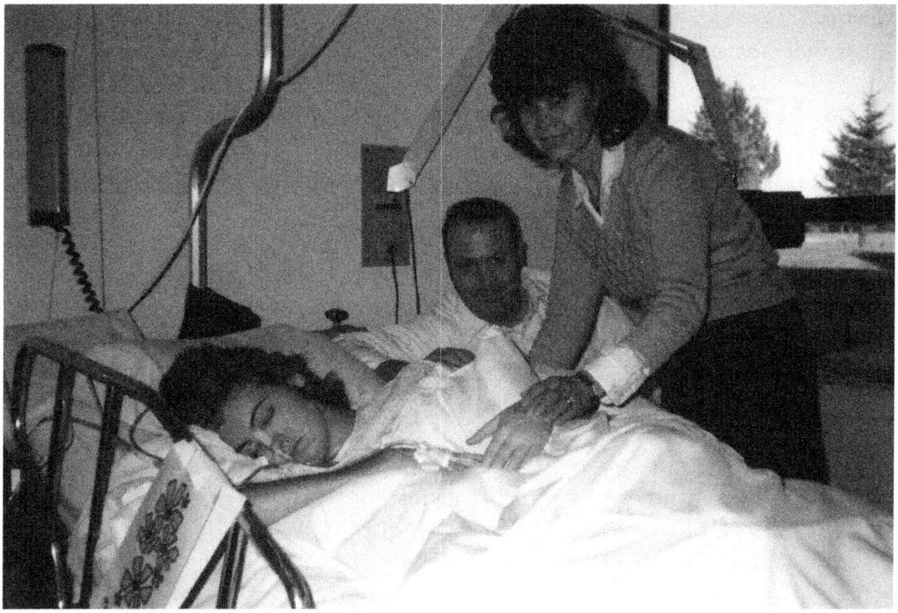

Mom showed up daily for almost four months.
Here she caught me sleeping.

Entertained by Angels

I like to say that during this time in my life, I was "entertained by angels." The phrase comes from the Bible, Hebrews 13:2: "Don't forget to show hospitality to strangers, for some who have done this have entertained angels without realizing it." In church, people often used the phrase to mean that we never can know who might bring us the grace of heaven.

Of course, I had literally encountered beings on the other side, whom I call angels, when I left my body. But now I'm talking about all the people who showed up to help me through the tricky process of recovery.

When I looked at these people, my angels, I could see clearly that none of them had so-called perfect personalities. Their quirks had served and saved me.

To start with, the self-described "by-the-book hard ass" John, my paramedic, had not given a damn about anyone else's opinion of my state. He took charge of the accident scene his way, and I thanked God for that.

Then Dr. Stewart stepped in when I needed her most. I believe the brilliance and tenacity which got her through med school at a time when a woman had to fight for her place also got me through some abysmal odds.

Nurse Sandy's self-professed obsessive-compulsive disorder type tendencies meant I received the best, most detailed care that anyone in my condition could hope for. God had brought her to this work for sure.

Captain Jan, a young woman with many cares of her own, had given everything she had to our friendship. Without hesitation, she had housed my mother, too. Her many visits and prayers gave my young heart a dose of normalcy, something that surely helped keep me here as much as the medical interventions.

And my mom. She devoted herself zealously to her religion during this time in a way that I would find challenging to deal with in years to come. Still, I know that her powerful faith had carried both of us. Mom had earned the right to claim as her own the Bible verse Isaiah 40:31: "But those who wait on the Lord shall renew their strength. They shall mount up with wings like eagles. They shall run and not be weary; they shall walk and not faint."

What is an angel, then? These beings of light and service have taken many forms: Archangels, guardian angels, military angels, healing angels. I could not list them all here.

I have encountered another kind of angel, too. It's you. It's me. Any one of us has the potential to make a profound difference in someone's life. I don't mean someday, once we finally get all our issues sorted out and become our ideal selves. I'm talking about now, today, as we are.

In Hawaii, I had begun to make some peace with what happened that day in Colorado. The healing work I had done made enough space inside of me to appreciate more deeply everything that had come together to keep me here on this side of the veil—everything and everyone.

CHAPTER 10: THE WHEEL TURNS AGAIN

Lesson 10:
*We will see loved ones and others when we return "home."**

August 2015

Three-thirty p.m. I am leaving the Adventist Health Castle hospital where I work, walking up the hill to the parking lot when I suddenly feel my chest constrict. I can hear myself gasping for air.

Uh oh, I think, as I stop beside my car to rest. Something isn't right.

My mind flashes ahead. In just six and a half hours, Paul and I will be getting on a plane. We are going on our long-overdue honeymoon (eleven years), an Alaskan cruise through the North Passage and then exploring Mt. Denali. I invited my parents to come to Hawaii to house sit for the two weeks we'll be gone, their own chance for the honeymoon they never had.

Paul and I have already rescheduled this trip once. A year earlier, a four month mainly non-stop migraine headache had kept us from traveling. Back then, I had to go on temporary disability at work while my neurologist tried methadone and a new anti-seizure med to get me better—a gruesome but ultimately successful experiment that broke the cycle.

I can't miss this trip again, dang it! But if my breathing is this labored now, how in the world will I make it to Alaska?

Winded, I climbed into my car for the quick seven-mile drive to my house. Once in the driveway, I sat with my head slumped over the wheel. I felt disoriented. I wanted to throw up.

---

* Source: https://mcusercontent.com/6aeb61681f6c311e999fff730/files/5070a118-63b3-4ac3-87f4-08b4f5d6e2e0/2020_IANDS_Annual_Report.01.pdf pg. 15

Finally, I mustered the energy to go inside and head for my bedroom. I hadn't even packed. All week I'd been dragging, too tired to take care of this essential task. But even now, with so little time left, I couldn't get myself motivated to do it.

"What's wrong?" Paul asked from the bedroom door.

"I don't feel good," I muttered. "Nauseous. Something doesn't seem right. I think we'd better go to the outpatient lab and get my blood drawn to check if my sodium levels are okay."

A few days ago, my doctor increased the dosage of a medication for diabetes insipidus (not to be confused with diabetes mellitus). I'm not sure my system is handling the change well.

"We'll be back soon," I told my parents as Paul and I rushed out the door.

I slumped into the car. About a mile from the hospital, Paul took a look at me and said, "I'm taking you to the E.R. instead. They'll get the results sooner and can treat you right there if there's a problem. Then we can still get on the plane."

My head nodded slowly up and down.

But once in the ER bed, all my symptoms were escalating. A nurse stepped into the little curtained area where we waited. Soon, the room filled with medical personnel, all of them tending to me.

"Nicole, I am sorry to say it, but you are not going anywhere except to a room upstairs in the main hospital. Your sodium level is critically low. The hospitalist will be down shortly to talk to you."

Huge tears streamed down my face. Once again, my health is keeping me—and Paul—from going to Alaska, having fun, living life.

Kindly the nurse pointed out that it's much better for me to find this out now than on a cruise ship. She's right, of course. But right now, I am inconsolable.

When the hospitalist arrives, he explains they are going to give me a peripherally inserted central catheter better known as a PICC line so they can draw my blood more easily along with giving me IV medications. It doesn't sound good.

I am suffering from hyponatremia, a condition of critically low sodium at the cellular level. If my sodium gets too low, I could die. If it rises too quickly, I could wind up paralyzed.

While I am being admitted, Paul runs back home to pick up a few things for me. He also tells my dad to move up their flight as soon as possible to avoid any cancellation fees. We need them to either go to a hotel or head back to the mainland now. Given all we are dealing with, Paul and I will need our home back as soon as possible. For one thing, I'll need to spend all my energy on recovery when I return home, not on entertaining guests. Also, we'll need our kitchen back. Since they arrived, my parents have commandeered the space while preparing meals according to the dictates of their latest epiphany to follow an Adventist Health vegetarian diet. Neither Paul nor I take any issue with the healthy diet. But since they've been staying with us, they have filled the kitchen from one end to the other with chopped vegetables from Costco, cooking three times a day. They would eat dinner promptly at 4:30 pm and we waited for them to finish every meal before we could prepare any food for ourselves. I could not believe this was my mom who used to love preparing food for us. In the whole four weeks they were with us she prepared two of my favorite meals (biscuits and chicken and dumplings) and they were sadly not as good as what I remembered. Now that I'm dealing with a health crisis, though, this just won't work. Paul needs unimpeded access to the kitchen to prepare food that I might be able to keep down.

In my first few days in the hospital, my sodium levels swing wildly. Monitors beep incessantly. Numerous staff bustle in and out of the room, endlessly checking my vital signs. They have the precarious task of boosting my sodium levels while simultaneously avoiding a too-rapid escalation that could paralyze me.

Throughout the ordeal, Paul stayed by my side most of the day, running out for a few hours each afternoon to deal with any loose threads at work and home. During these interim periods, my parents made a few visits, refusing to hop a plane to go see my sister. Their behavior definitely fell short of what I had hoped given my dire condition. When they showed up, since I worked there, they met and spent most of their time with the hospital president's executive secretary (who stopped in to see me), a woman who served as a kind of missionary to the facility and community. They made no effort to hide their lack of interest in me. When Paul returned, they left. Paul slept every night in a recliner the staff provided.

It took the doctors some time to get my condition sorted. Five days, to be exact. Not what I had in mind when I told my parents I would be back soon.

When I finally arrived home my dad greeted me. He and my mother had had plenty of time to arrange a flight home and make their exit. But our request had fallen on deaf ears. Knowing how challenging the situation would be, Paul wanted to insist that they leave. But I just couldn't handle it right then. I didn't have the energy to stand up to my parents in my condition.

And at least my dad was talking to me. On our arrival, Mom stayed in the kitchen, without so much as a hello. I headed straight to bed.

The next morning, I found that walking the twenty-five feet from my bedroom to our kitchen left me completely winded, my chest tight and breathing shallow. "My God, what has happened to me?" I thought.

Things didn't change much over the next few days. I found myself more or less collapsing any time I stood to walk, even though I was resting. Could I have heart problems? Granted, I hadn't eaten much in the last few months. Persistent forceful belching—every time I ate—had sent me to a gastrointestinal specialist. A diagnosis of candida yeast of the esophagus prompted a high dose of meds and a very low-sugar and yeast-free diet. I had lost a lot of weight, already too much. Back down to the low 120's (from a healthier 135 lbs.).

Not an ideal state, physically speaking, for a week-long stay at the hospital. I would even call it hell, except that I had already endured even worse at age 19. That week, though, a week with my parents in the house, made me think I had it easy in the hospital. There I faced physical dangers. At home, I was living through an emotional nightmare.

Since coming home, my mother had devoted most of her communication with me to snipes, barbs, and blatant criticism.

"You're so skinny. You must be anorexic!" she swats.

Yes, Mom, I have just suffered months of constant migraine headaches that have made food completely unappealing. On top of that, I deal with major issues with my gut. Every time I eat, I get horrible bloating and belching. Oh, and you may remember that I have just spent a week in the hospital. Not exactly known for its gourmet food options.

All of this commentary remains inside my head, though. I yearn for Mom to comfort me. Soothe me. Approve of me. If I upset her, she never will. If I keep quiet, maybe she'll relent.

But of course, she doesn't. Instead, she launches into some of her favorite refrains.

"What did you do to bring this illness on yourself?" Or "If you would only accept Jesus and get rid of that awful Buddha wall hanging..."

All of this came to a head one afternoon. Paul had left the house. Mom waits to wage her most direct attacks on me when he leaves. She, my father, and I were sitting at the kitchen table together.

Mom starts with, "It's really your fault, Nicole. You're sick again because of that Buddha statue on your mantelpiece."

Me: Silence.

"And you're not a Christian."

"What makes you think I'm not a Christian?" I ask defensively.

"Because you don't go to church," she snaps back.

"Yes," I tell her, "I do go to church, Mom."

"What church?" she badgers.

"The Church of the Beach."

"That's not a church. I can spot a Christian, Nicole, and you are not one."

"Okay, Mom, so you're telling me that Jesus said, 'Judge not, lest you be judged,' but you're judging me because I'm not going to a church with four walls and a ceiling?"

"That's right," she jabs without a moment's hesitation. "And you did this to yourself, too, making yourself sick and anorexic." And she leans hard on her next words. "You're not beautiful anymore."

With that she gets up from her chair. Stunned, I can do little more than stare at her retreating back. Did she really just say that?

Finally, I found my voice. "Dad, do you believe what she just said?"

"Well," he answers me, "you look better."

If Paul had been home, I know he would have kicked them out of the house then and there. When he returned, I didn't tell him.

With all this going on, my condition was not improving to say the least. In the week since I left the hospital, I had dropped another ten pounds and still could barely walk.

Paul, very concerned, took me back to the hospital for a scheduled appointment with the G.I. doc. All my tests came back normal, though. The doctor can't make sense of it.

Then out of nowhere, I am hyperventilating.

The room grew dark around me. Nausea washed through me, and I felt shaky. The G.I. doctor sat me in a wheelchair and rolled me to the ER in the next building. He was concerned I was having a heart attack.

Then the symptoms truly escalated.

But when the ER doctors ran multiple tests, all of them came back normal.

"What's going on at home, Nicole? Anything besides the obvious stressing you out?" the compassionate ER doctor asked me.

I mentioned that my parents were staying with us and that my mom was haranguing me about my so-called godlessness. Paul's head nearly exploded when he heard this.

The doctor responded. "Nicole, you're having an anxiety attack. I'm giving you Ativan to calm you down and a script for Valium to take later as needed. But I think it's probably time for your parents to go home. You need some time away from them. You may want to consider going into therapy, too, to deal with those relationships."

Of course, Paul wanted them gone immediately. He was ready to confront them as soon as we got home. But I knew he couldn't be the one to do it. They would never forgive him.

When I arrived home, I told my parents we needed to have a talk. My mother said she would be ready in half an hour, and we had to come to her room. Paul put me in our bed where I promptly sank into the mattress. He informed my parents that the meeting would be in our bedroom. Mom refused to be a part of it. So, I explained to my father that I needed time and space to heal.

"Dad, I just had an anxiety attack related to the stress of my relationship with Mom. I need you to control her and her negative behavior towards me." Paul added that if he couldn't do that, then they would have to find a hotel for the remaining few days till their flight.

Dad told me he couldn't control Mom, but he would speak to her.

Get out! I wanted to scream at him. But I didn't scream.

I tried to explain this away. I told myself that I was tired, so tired. Too weary to kick them out. Deep down, though, I knew the truth was a lot more complicated.

Inside, I am still a child. Still afraid of my parents' disapproval. And still desperate for my mother's love.

My parents stayed for another few tension-filled days. Even when their presence was nearly killing me, I couldn't bring myself to stand up to them.

Stages of Grief

In the last chapter, I shared a lot of details about how my mother cared for me after my car accident. Her dedication to my well-being back then astounds me, even now. I know how much she sacrificed to make sure I lived.

She relied heavily on religion to get through that time. And her approach did have a genuinely spiritual component. Constantly she turned to God, talking to Him like her best friend. I believe God became real for her then. Her faith became real, too. She put me on prayer lists around the world and prayed constantly herself. During that time, she saw miracles.

One of the many difficult days Mom lived through after the accident comes to mind. I had taken a sudden, sharp turn for the worse. Dr. Brown, a highly capable expert on infections from Denver was unable to diagnose two of the three major infections attacking my system. Machine bells went off like crazy, the nurses rushed in to prep me for emergency surgery. Mom and my father, who happened to be there at the time, retreated to the chapel to pray as Dr. Stewart rushed to the O.R. to perform surgery.

From her pew, Mom heard over the intercom system, "Code Blue in OR 1! Code Blue in OR 1!" She locked eyes with my dad. They knew immediately the intercom was talking about me.

Just then, a surgical nurse rushed into the chapel. "Mr. and Mrs. Kerr, Nicole arrested on the table. The doctors have lost her. They tried everything to save her, but she has died. I am so sorry."

In response, my father began to cry. Mom had never before seen him do this. "We have to make a decision now," he told her through tears. "Where are we going to bury her?"

But my mom came back with, "I am not going there. I am not giving up. I do not believe she is dead."

It turned out Mom was right.

Of course, someone looking at the situation intellectually, from a psychological lens, could point out that denial is the first stage of grief for everyone. My mom had entered that stage.

And that's where things got a bit tricky. In my heart, I know that more than just denial was operating for her. I think her intuition was telling her that I had not yet left. I would be off base to reduce her experience down to boilerplate psychobabble.

On the other hand, I also don't love everything about the way moments like these have impacted my mom. They did not just reinforce her faith in God. They also reinforced her rigid views on religion. The things she witnessed in my recovery did not create a deeper relationship with the loving God I had encountered as our Oneness. Rather, they entrenched her ever more deeply in the harsh, judgmental deity her religion espouses so zealously.

Does that mean all those prayers said for me by Christians around the world did not have an impact on my recovery? Absolutely not. I know that prayer works—no matter what religion it springs from. Why? In spirit, we are one. Any loving, positive intention you send toward another person reaches them, and you, instantly.

But the issue? Prayer doesn't have to look a certain way, follow a set pattern. In my own experience, the most profound prayers I have experienced have arisen from within me in the space of silence. I think of true prayer as communion with Source. Anyone, anywhere, at any time can accomplish this. No one religion has the "real" line to God.

During my time in the hospital at age nineteen, another thing happened. My mother made an agreement with God. If I survived, she would become a "missionary" for Him.

Using the Kübler-Ross model, experts in grief call this bargaining. It's another classic feature of the grieving process, something that people from every culture around the world experience. Experts have labeled it the third stage of grief (though many acknowledge that people move through the stages differently). In an effort to feel less out of control in the face of death, we try to cut a deal with God or the world. (For more on the grief journey, check out the work of Elisabeth Kübler-Ross.)

Mom interpreted my survival to mean that God had signed her proposed contract on the dotted line. She took it seriously. Almost four decades later, she actively attends two protestant churches and spends many hours a day in prayer and Bible study. When not doing this, she watches the Jesus channel and preaches to anyone who will listen (and plenty who won't).

All of this I can stomach. I have respect for anyone's devotion to God. The dogmatic judgment she lives by, though ... that's what I find so hard to handle. Mom has used it to erect a barrier between herself and me, as well as most of the rest of the world.

I can see how much unresolved trauma has fed her obsessive relationship with religion. I know from her descriptions what a harrowing experience she had after my accident. At that time, she gave and gave and gave, without a way to refill her own tanks. This she had endured not long after my older sister had almost died from a horseback riding accident. Not long after my crash, my brother survived a serious military truck accident at Quantico that left another Marine dead and several forever disabled.

Apart from her religious fervor, my mom has never sought support to heal from any of these harrowing experiences. Her horrific childhood, also never addressed, would have only made these life-threatening situations her children endured even worse. How much grief Mom must carry around inside herself all the time, never given expression.

I think of unexpressed griefs as a long chain. One grief links to another, and that one to another, and so forth. Pull on one, and all the others come. Blaming me for my health problems during her visit in Hawaii must have seemed internally like the only way she could handle her own string of suppressed griefs. Her nervous system must have been swamped by painful feelings she could not process.

Whether or not Mom knew it, she had also made me a part of her deal with God so many years ago. God, her God, had done so much for me. How dare I go against Him now? I believe that when Mom lashed out at me during her Hawaii visit, she was, in her own mind, fulfilling her role as a parent. In her own mind, she was well within her rights to punish me for wrongdoing. That's how it works when you live in the shadow of a punishing God. You have to pay, and so does everyone else.

Maybe, too, Mom was getting me back for all the sacrifices she made. After that, I owed her my unquestioning allegiance. Right? I owed her my life. My beliefs. All my choices.

I shared in an earlier chapter that everything in ourselves that we do not face, we will project onto others. My mother's behavior toward me offers a clear example. Instead of feeling her own pain, she found a way to make me hurt. It probably did make her feel better, superficially and for a moment. But it didn't resolve her own hurt.

More Understanding

You may remember from previous chapters that we unconsciously recreate and relive traumatic memories until we finally resolve them. Now, with my parents close by, I had found myself in the hospital once again, and at death's door.

Going through this experience as an adult, with many years on my own, I began to understand for the first time how much my mother's attention had meant to me in the hospital so many years ago. Until the accident, I had ranked pretty low in the family hierarchy. My needs came after my two younger brothers, because they were boys, and my sister, because she was older and prettier. In an effort to get some measure of affection and attention, I became a people pleaser. Ironically, my strategy ultimately backfired. I never upset anyone, but I also never got much attention, either. I never made waves, and never asked for much.

Then I almost died. For four solid months (and eight months in physical therapy afterwards), my mother spent her energy on nothing but me and my needs. Finally I felt loved—or at least something like it. No, my mom was not seeing and appreciating me for who I was. But at least she was noticing me and giving me her undivided focus for the first time.

But now, even though I couldn't bring myself to kick her out of my house, I was still refusing to please her by refusing to go along with her rules and religion. And she was rolling up her sleeves to put the first nail in my coffin.

This chilling awareness helped me grasp how much I truly had needed to become a pleaser as a child to survive. Compassion for myself was growing from this difficult encounter with my parents.

Honolulu Airport, just before Thanksgiving 2015

"Daryl? Daryl, is that you?" I ask.

"OMG, Nicole! How are you?" Daryl answers. She's a fellow registered dietitian whom I've known for years. "Where are you headed?"

"San Diego," I answered. After the stress of the last few months, Paul and I really needed a vacation.

My self-confidence had hit an all-time low after my parents left. At first Paul had to drive me everywhere since I felt so shaky and unsure of myself. Thirty-two years after my car crash, and back to baby steps. Drive one mile up the road. Yeah, I made it. Then drive to my friend's home five miles away. Okay, made that, too. Drive to work, six miles away. Pretty soon I could function again. I started back to work part-time, but I got tired easily. In all I had lost thirteen pounds and weighed in at 120, extremely low for my 5'11" frame. Doctors still could not figure out why I wasn't getting better and gaining weight. In mid-November one doctor suggested I go to the mainland for an evaluation. Paul and I were taking his advice. We also intended to rest and play.

"I'm headed to San Diego, too," Daryl tells me. "Looks like we're on the same flight."

After I met her son, we started talking shop. I ended up telling her about my health situation.

Casually she asks, "How many calories are you eating?"

"I don't know. Probably 1,500."

"Nicole, that is way too low for you. You should be at more like 3,000 calories a day. Maybe you should come in and see me. Think about it."

As we boarded our flight, I caught a glimpse of a beautiful rainbow through the plane window.

"Wow," I tell Daryl, pointing to the rainbow. "That is a sign from the angels that I was supposed to run into you."

Refeeding: The Irony of a Registered Dietician Being Malnourished

I made my first appointment with Daryl as soon as I returned. She helped me to understand that many of the symptoms I had suffered in the last year-and-a-half stemmed from protein malnutrition.

"Rest and eat whatever you want. Gain weight."

To a lot of people, this sounds like an enviable prescription. I found it a lot harder to do, though. As a Registered Dietitian Nutritionist with a master's degree in public health nutrition, I had advised many with similar issues, including people with clinical anorexia. I already knew I needed to increase my food gradually, to avoid the risk of knocking my phosphorus levels out of balance. But I found it a whole lot easier to tell others than to accomplish it myself. I had to start slowly, adding calories and foods a bit at a time. As usual, Paul helped tremendously, supporting me both in the kitchen, with finding the right foods, and in developing the emotional and mental strength to keep going. In the end, it took me a full six months to regain the weight.

During that time, I was doing more than just feeding my body. I was waking up to how little true nourishment my relationship with my parents had ever offered me. I also became starkly aware of how my drive to please them (and others) at all costs was a way of denying myself of nourishment.

Clearly, I had to do something about it all. Many people link that word "enlightenment" with the word "awakening." My parents' visit had given me a wake-up call, a chance to enlighten or lighten up another aspect of my personality.

From time to time, life offers moments like this one. Moments when you face a choice. On one level, you realize you must choose between staying in a comfort zone, where it's familiar and cozy—and, ahem, also toxic—or moving forward into the unknown, which looks terrifying as hell.

I've learned that these moments are, on another level, a choice between staying dead or deciding to live.

Of course, deciding to wake up and live in a part of your life where you've generally kept yourself numbed out, deadened, asleep, usually feels like stepping off a cliff. Or at the least, it can seem like you wandered off alone in the backcountry without a map. That's because, well, you don't have a map. You've never been here.

That's why I have found it incredibly helpful to get support from others who know the terrain. Sometimes I've had to fumble around for a while looking for the help I need. But it always comes. Serendipity arises from alignment. The support I got from my friend Daryl, who dropped into my life seemingly "out of nowhere," illustrates this beautifully. When I was committed to making a change, I opened myself up to the miracle.

And that miracle didn't stop with Daryl, either. In the time after my parents' visit, I met Dr. Dennis Rhatigan, a chiropractor and NET practitioner.

What is Healing?

My earliest encounters with NET amazed me. Dr. Rhatigan was using a tool that combines so many different facets of healing in one integrated process. It blends modern Western science with ancient Eastern traditions. It also addresses the impact of environmental toxicity, nutritional balance, and the body's structural integrity. And here's what I love most: It grounds everything in the context of emotional wellness.

At my first appointment with Dr. Rhatigan, I explained many of my physical symptoms: frequent urination, belching, migraines, etc. Instead of simply rattling off a list of supplements or pharmaceuticals I needed to buy, however, he wanted to talk about the emotional component of these physical issues. He pointed to my relationship with my mother. I had to face the fact that my mother cared more about herself and her beliefs than about my feelings or needs.

I can't say it felt great to hear all this. But it did feel true. I finally admitted to myself that I had to stop, once and for all, working constantly to please her. I had clung to the last threads of my old identity as the perfect daughter, even when it literally almost killed me! Facing all the negative emotions my relationship with my mother stirred up for me had terrified me that much.

NET was giving me a concrete way to access these issues, not just in my mind, but in and through the body. Remember that I've shared in earlier chapters how neurotransmitters can carry emotional messages throughout the body. NET focuses on finding these unresolved emotional stress patterns that have been lodged in the nervous system and physiology. Instead of going into mental mode to talk about the issue, NET goes straight to the body to learn what it has to say. It relies on muscle testing to check your body's ability to maintain congruent functioning in the presence of a potential emotional trigger and helps your body resolve the mind-body stress pattern.

NET showed me that my body could speak more clearly than my intellect when it came to my emotions. Then some simple techniques—simple, but not simplistic, since they are based on ancient medical wisdom—helped to clear and shift the old pattern. Years, even decades of stuck energy was starting to move for me. I could not doubt the power of this work.

And I'm not the only one. I'll share a study focused on NET and cancer diagnosis. Researchers at The Marcus Institute of Integrative Health at Thomas Jefferson University tested NET for efficacy in reducing symptoms of traumatic stress in cancer patients. The stress of receiving a cancer diagnosis can last long after even the last cancer treatment for many. In fact, the emotional trauma of a diagnosis can prove one of the hardest aspects of the disease. But the study showed a powerful positive impact on that stress by NET. "The results of this study were quite dramatic. In just four to five brief sessions, patients who received NET reported much less distress, their overall emotional state improved significantly and the way their brains reacted to stress cues normalized." *

The more time I spent with Dr. Rhatigan doing the NET healing work, the more I understood the importance of emotional and spiritual wellness in my own physical well-being. Don't get me wrong. I knew all this already, in theory. But NET was giving me a practical access point for my mental understanding to become embodied.

My decision to study NET myself marked a turning point in my growth. Since the car accident, I had constantly looked for an outside entity to fix me. I wanted someone, anyone, to step in and take charge. If I did everything my doctor, naturopath, therapist, chiropractor, etc. told me to do, then I would heal. But even the best remedies fail to heal old wounds for the person not connected to the Source of true healing, the God within.

When I learned NET, I learned to go within myself. I could access the mind-body axis inside me and use it to heal. I came to see that God, the God I had met beyond the veil, would guide me to the right healing practices if I listened carefully.

Patterns I spent a lifetime (many lifetimes?) developing did not disappear magically. At work I found myself still attempting to please my staff, despite very inappropriate behavior on their part. And maybe I wasn't achieving perfect health like I had dreamed. I still lived with migraines and other health challenges I would rather have ended. But I was experiencing more and more joy, less and less pain.

I was discovering the true nature of healing. All my life, I had thought of healing as curing. If I could go to a doctor and get rid of my condition, then, poof—healed! Now it was dawning on me that I could heal something on a deep level, whether or not I got cured of physical symptoms.

You've probably heard the adage, pain is mandatory, but suffering is optional. Pain happens on a physical level, to all of us. Suffering

* Source: https://www.ncbi.nlm.nih.gov/pubmed/28181091

results from your mental and emotional states. On a gorgeous day, with no clouds in the sky and nothing but good things happening in your life, you can still suffer. Maybe you worry about an unseen future, wring your hands in regret over an unchangeable past, or yearn desperately for something you don't have. Someone else, your next-door neighbor, say, could be dying from cancer. Yet she is living in bliss, focused on gratitude and her connection with all of life.

Healing, true healing was arising in my life as I released myself from the prisons I had created for myself.

September 2021

In the wee hours of the morning, I found myself awake. I was not alone, though. My mother was there.

The encounter began as my morning meditation. I was sitting in bed, focused inward. Then a pair of chocolate eyes, a cute pug nose, and dark brown hair appeared in my mind's eye. My mother's face.

"Nicole, I am so sorry that I was not there for you. That I missed seeing your pain. That I listened to your father instead of listening to myself, that I turned on you, judged you, pressured you. I could not find a way to show you unconditional love. Please forgive me. Know that who I truly am, my Soul and Spirit, does love you and accept you. Always has and always will. Remember that no matter what else happens in the physical realm, this is who I really am. Try to understand that I lost myself a long time ago. "

Tears rushed down my cheeks.

Finally, I understood my mother. Not just intellectually, but through the lens of my heart. What she went through those four months in the hospital with me. Wondering whether or not I would live, and even if I did, what my condition would be in the long term. All of it, on top of the madness of her own childhood, had traumatized her anew.

With the benefit of this insight, I can see why she treated me so harshly when she came to our home. I had betrayed her. That's how it felt to her, anyway. She had given everything she had. But I hadn't adhered to her beliefs, which felt like a stab in the back to her. Is that fair to me? No. I never made any agreement with her or her God. Does it make sense? Well, not rationally. But when are feelings ever rational? My mom could not see past her own limiting beliefs... just like me. How many times had my own limits gotten in the way of my giving unconditional love to those closest to me? More than I could count, I'm sure.

My mind wandered back to what Mom had told the AFA doctor when he suggested I see a psychologist. "God and Jesus are our therapists. We don't need any other help." Sadness washed over me. I knew how much psychotherapy had supported me to recover from trauma. If only my mother had been able to receive the same support.

Later that evening, I found myself on a zoom call with my parents and siblings, organized to connect with my sister, whose son's wedding none of us could attend. For the first time in four years, I saw my mother, even if only on a computer screen.

And I felt the peace that passes all understanding.

The Healing Journey

I look back on the events of the latter part of 2015 and think, man, that really took it out of me. I was reliving so many aspects of the car accident. Once again, I found myself hospitalized with a life-or-death condition. Worse, my parents attacked me with judgment, just like the first time. And if I'm honest, I still felt like I had done something to deserve it all.

Not everything perfectly mirrored the past, though. This time I knew my parents' judgments of me did not line up with God's opinion. Even if a part of me still agreed with them, another part most definitely did not. That part of me, the one I had spent so many years reclaiming, would help me achieve a level of healing I never had before. I was strong enough now to use the crisis to transform myself. That's what I've been doing ever since the first accident. Still, it happened this time with so much more ease. I went further, faster.

Over the years, this marks my own experience of healing. First, I take baby steps. Then, as my strength increases, I can accomplish more. Like all of us, I have had moments (sometimes years) of discouragement. At times, healing has looked less like a journey to me and more like a dead end. But even in all my searching, the times when it felt like I was getting nowhere, I was making progress. Along the way, I was building incredible empathy for anyone working through challenges with their health.

Perhaps you already know of Biblical accounts when Jesus healed people. More than once he said, "Your faith has made you well." Now that I understand more about healing, I especially appreciate the King James Version of one of these encounters. He said to a woman, "Thy faith hath made thee whole."

Yes, whole. Wholeness rings true. Healing comes when I remember who I truly am as Source. But it doesn't stop there. It also arises from accepting who I am here. All of me. My messy mistakes, my missteps, and even the misfortunes I create. Healing comes through that kind of embrace.

In this lifetime, I will never again feel my mother's arms physically wrapping around me in a loving way. She is still alive and lives outside of Melbourne, Australia, where their business, Red Roo Manufacturing, Inc. is located. But the love has been replaced with coldness and disappointment. The thought brings tears, even now. She has confused disappointment with dishonor in all of her children. Still, I know I am held, deeply, eternally, in the arms of the Great Mother who holds us all. My own arms become hers as I grow into my divine self, a little more every day.

CHAPTER 11: FULL CIRCLE

Lesson 11:
*Our true selves are perfect, and we are loved more than we can fathom.**

In 2021, after years of renting, Paul and I purchased a new house—well, really, an old one, historic, built in 1850. About ten years ago, the previous owners stripped it to the studs and remodeled it, so we know it's in great condition. Our new-old (old-new?) house ticks lots of other boxes, too: beautiful, roomy, in the historical part of downtown we love, and a short walk to everywhere we enjoy going. Almost magically, we have landed in a space that meets and even exceeds our expectations.

Here's what we did not expect about buying this house: just about everything!

For starters, we came to look at it casually, the day it went up for sale. On Friday we hired a realtor. On Sunday we were able to see the house before anyone else. Within two hours we had made an offer, before a "For Sale" sign had even been put in the yard.

For another thing, I never—and when I say never, I mean *never*—expected to find myself living in New Bern, North Carolina. This little Hallmark town lies just thirty-three miles from where I was born, Camp Lejeune Marine Corp Base. If you had told me, even just a handful of years ago, that I would land here, I would have laughed in your face. Talk about coming full circle in your life.

Shoot, at my age, I never expected to find myself buying another house, period, new, old, or otherwise. Paul and I have started to enter our "golden years" and should be simplifying our lives. Letting go. Downsizing. Like we did when we left Hawaii during the midst of the pandemic in June of 2020, right?

---

* Source: https://mcusercontent.com/6aeb61681f6c311e999fff730/files/5070a118-63b3-4ac3-87f4-08b4f5d6e2e0/2020_IANDS_Annual_Report.01.pdf pg. 15

Recently Paul joked with me about a few of his previous attitudes about life after retirement:

1. Buy a house. NO!
2. Buy a big house. HELL NO!
3. Buy a big, old house. A THOUSAND TIMES, OH HELL NO!

And yet, here we are. The script I had written inside my head for this stage of my life looked nothing like this. Instead of whiling the hours away at my knitting (no, I don't actually knit), I find myself busily shopping for furniture.

Paul and I moved here with almost nothing. When we left Hawaii, we sold everything except clothing, art we cherished, a single box of Christmas ornaments, a bookshelf Paul had made, and his guitars. We boiled down our collective 120 years of material acquisitions to just forty boxes and a prayer.

Now I find myself not just in a new state but on a whole new continent (or a new-old one, if you like, since I have lived on it before). Instead of the warm, aloha Pacific, I now wake each day just a few miles from the chillier Atlantic coast. Nothing about this place resembles anything of my life in Hawaii.

What a relief, too. Unlike my existence in Hawaii as a *haole*, where I dealt daily with the prickly stares of locals, the removed questions of tourists, and the revolving door of people who intended to stay, but then didn't, this warm little place has embraced Paul and me with open, stable arms. We've already made the front page of the newspaper with the headline, "Our Goal is to be Real Contributors." I've met more people socially in less than two years than I had in all my time in Hawaii. People here go out of their way to greet Paul and me on our daily walks with the dogs.

Oh, right—the dogs. Yet another thing I never expected. I'm sure Paul would have put them on his "HELL NO" list, too, before we got them. A friend we met during our first six months here had invited us over to "furniture shop" from his home. He would soon be moving, too. Instead of furniture, though, we walked away with two five-year-old Pekingese pooches. We had become acquainted with the owner and dogs as the trio did their daily walks around the neighborhood. When we took the dogs, he said he had planned to put them up for adoption the next morning. Instead, the dynamic brother-sister duo, Bella and Beaux, moved into our new house the day after we did. Never before have I owned or even aspired to own a dog. But these two adopted us, not the other way around. What a lovely addition they have made to our family!

Everything about our new-old life has surprised me. How great that nothing has gone according to my plans!

Paradigm Shift

Maybe it sounds like I found a geographic cure. You know, that hope we all secretly cherish that moving to a new place will give us an amazing new life, without all the hassles and problems that currently plague us.

Though, it has happened the other way around for me. For a while now, I have been brewing up big changes internally. Everything happening outside simply reflects them. My way of seeing the world has shifted so dramatically that I can only call it a paradigm shift.

To understand what I mean by paradigm, consider the many different aspects of personality that I've covered. Ego identities, unconscious beliefs, projections, patterns, brain chemistry, and more. All of that stuff comes together, both to create and to keep in place the paradigm you live from. Your paradigm has many facets, all of which show up in the details of your daily life.

Now reflect on what happens when your paradigm shifts. Maybe one day you realize that some belief you've cherished your whole life has no basis in reality. When you pull on that thread, you don't know what other aspects of your outlook might connect with it. In a short time, you can find your whole world unraveling.

My choice to leave behind the church of my childhood, for instance, marks one of my own major paradigm shifts. This shift put me on a journey toward deeper spiritual understanding that even now I have not completed. In this lifetime, I doubt I will. And this change in my fundamental way of seeing the world has sparked a host of other paradigm shifts for me over the years.

In ancient Egyptian myth, the Sun God Ra descended every night through the twelve gates of the underworld. For morning to come, he would have to ascend through them in reverse. At times, my own journey since the accident feels like this. Because of that experience, I descended into the depths of myself. Now I am re-emerging. Along the way I pass through so many different territories. And sometimes I move through not just scenery but a gate. On the other hand, the landscape looks entirely different. My life changes noticeably.

My new life in North Carolina illustrates the way an internal paradigm shift can help us manifest big changes externally. Here's another anecdote to shed more light on what I mean.

For years I have dealt with the Veterans Administration (VA). I had filed multiple disability claims over the decades for the many injuries I suffered in the accident and their ongoing symptoms. In large part, the VA has, over time, come to agree with me. The organization has gradually raised the rating to 90%. (As a side note, I will share that in my own mind, I don't like to call this "disability," but rather, compensation. And I have appreciated every dollar of compensation I have received.)

Still, something niggled. Of all the medical conditions I have dealt with to date, the migraine headaches have disabled me far more than any other. I have lived with them every week, and I never quite know when one will come. Along these lines, doctors have now established a clear link between PTSD and migraines. Anyone living with PTSD understands this. The condition causes the body to live in a heightened state of stress and sensitivity. But even though the VA has acknowledged in my claim that I live with PTSD, it has refused to acknowledge that the migraines have any correlation to my injuries. Never mind the fact that I never had a migraine before the car accident. Since no doctor during my initial hospital treatments ever wrote in my medical record, "head injury" or "traumatic brain injury (TBI)" the VA doctors reviewing my claims would not admit the problem had come from my injuries.

Over the years I've tried everything within my power to get them to understand this. I have had multiple exams by new doctors who link the migraines with the accident. I've pointed to the pages and pages of my case notes that show the severity of the migraines as well as their onset after the crash. I've jumped through all the hoops.

Ultimately, my frustration with the situation has come less from lost dollars than from a sense of feeling invisible. Did the people reviewing my claim even take time to look at my file? At one point they admitted they did not. Do they have any idea what I live with every day? Do they even care?

It sounds a lot like how I've felt with my parents. Of course, I have always felt I was invisible to them. Only more recently, though, did I come to understand this. My interactions with my mother in Hawaii when she attacked me for "heresy" brought it to a head. How could she be so callous? Did she ever really see me as a person, or just an extension of herself? Did she care about me at all?

In the years since that visit, I have spent many hours on questions like these. They have dredged up a lot of pain for me. More sessions with my NET practitioner than I can count have pointed to my need to stop looking for my mother's approval in my life. Would I ever be able to do this?

The answer is, "Yes."

I have worked to get myself to that yes, though. Even though the process hurts sometimes, I haven't given up on my commitment to heal from the pain sparked by my relationship with my mother.

Along the way, I have discovered some things which surprised me. As well as the resentment and anger I have carried toward my mother, I recently unearthed the anger I have felt toward my father all these years. How dare he push me to go to the Academy, a brutal place, not right for me in any way? It had nearly caused my death, and ruined the life left to me. His job as my father was to consider my welfare. My needs. Did he even care about me at all, or only himself?

As I allowed these feelings to move through me, I found myself accessing an even deeper layer of emotion. Fury rose in me, not toward my parents, but myself.

Yes, my parents had dumped me at the AFA. When I had called home at the three-week mark of basic cadet training (we each got a three-minute phone call) I heard my mother's voice say "Hello" and that was it for me. I proceeded to hyperventilate, sobbing uncontrollably, and actually could not speak for the entire call, my first panic attack. My mother could not understand what was going on, but I could not say that I wanted to quit, to please let me come home. The officer said my time was up and told me to sit over on the side and get myself together. Mom told me later that she asked my father, "What have we done to her?" He stated I would be fine and that was the end of it. I was anything but fine. I thought, "It is too late now. I have to do it." My fate had been sealed since I didn't get another phone call till Parents' Weekend, another three weeks away. Then I would see them in person.

But I was the one, not her, who had stayed there anyway. I had chosen to attend the AFA to please my dad, even though just over a single year there had nearly destroyed me.

What an idiot I'd been. I had played the fool. I had betrayed myself. For this, I did not just feel angry. I actually hated myself.

Needless to say, I did a lot of crying as all these feelings surfaced. Letting myself touch these emotions went against every instinct in me. Yet doing this was exactly the right medicine. Embracing the pain helped it to finally leave my system.

Ironically, what I most wanted, to be seen, was what I first had to give to myself. By accepting and loving myself more fully, I could also forgive and accept my mother more fully. The more I approved of myself, the less I needed approval from her. I even had plenty left over to give away.

What a profound internal shift. And something has happened externally, too.

When I got to North Carolina, I connected with my local VA rep. He felt I had a strong claim and encouraged me to make one more appeal for the final 10% of disability the VA could grant.

The whole thing made me nervous, of course. It would be my third appeal; the final one I could make. If it went wrong, I would not have another chance. On the other hand, I would accomplish nothing if I did nothing.

My rep gave me great support. He helped me understand the power of saying less, not more, about my condition, since the doctors reviewing it see thousands of claims. We needed to show them, very clearly and from the original case notes, the link between the migraines and the accident. So, he used one simple phrase from the very earliest part of my medical record as the foundation of my final appeal.

"Patient thought to be dead at the scene."

When I went online to check the status of this final appeal months later, my hands were shaking. But I'm sure you've figured out by now where this is going.

The VA granted me its highest rating for the migraines. I would receive the final 10% of my claim thus raising my rating to 100% permanent disability for the rest of my life.

When I saw this decision, I cried, this time not from hurt, but joy and relief. When I saw a deposit in our bank account which confirmed it, I cried again. The long years of struggling to prove myself had come to an end.

On the other side of all this, I knew, not intellectually, but in my bones, that the AFA and the car accident had not ruined me. These experiences had made me.

Now I am living in an entirely new world.

My Story and I'm Stickin' to It

I'm always amazed at how often we think we've left behind a negative belief or pattern, only to find it resurfacing in a different way.

One of my biggest catalysts for my most recent personal transformation has been writing this book. For at least a few decades, I knew I needed to write about the car accident and its impact. Yet I never quite knew how. Finally, I just rolled up my sleeves and got started.

For a while I really was stuck. It took a while for me to understand what the book needed to say. I kept thinking I would write a book about how I had miraculously used the power in my mind to heal every ailment in my body—and how you could, too.

I suppose I was comparing myself to other people, authors who have had NDEs or other writers who have created miraculous physical healing for themselves. Unconsciously I believed that until I did the same, I didn't have a worthy story to tell.

Luckily, I kept going. The more I worked on the book, the more I understood what the book wanted to teach me. I was discovering what I had to say by saying it.

Fairly deep into the project, I had a big revelation. I was writing about some of my ongoing health challenges and how I was creating, or at least prolonging, those problems. I had learned this pattern in my childhood, I reasoned, as a way to get out of doing stuff I didn't want to, like going to church. Now I was still creating health problems for myself. One plus one equals two, over and done. I needed to break through my old pattern of seeing sickness as an easy out if I wanted to get well.

Then I showed the writing to a friend.

"Nicole," she told me, "I think you're really being tough on yourself. Your body has been through so much. Your nervous system is weaker than other peoples, and it's not just in your head. Maybe you can be more tender with yourself. More generous."

That's when it hit me. After all this time I was still finding ways to blame myself for the car accident. I had dressed it all up in New Age clothes, of course. No longer was I telling myself that I deserved the accident because God was punishing me for disobeying my father.

Now I was saying to myself something like, I'm still sick because I haven't worked hard enough at healing myself yet. When I am finally more enlightened, I will no longer deal with any health challenges. When I finally heal all the migraines, for example, or, say, overcome the panic attacks, only then do I deserve to accept my body. And finally, my story will really matter. Until that time, I'd better push myself to heal.

What an oxymoron. I still cowered in the shadow of an angry God, one that only existed in my unconscious mind, of course. And I wasn't giving myself permission to live, right here and right now. Instead, I was using my health issues as evidence of God's disapproval of me.

Don't misunderstand me. I do fully believe in the power of the higher mind to heal the body. I know we can create greater and greater health in our lives through our thoughts, beliefs, and habitual emotions. The NET mind-body stress relief work I do with client's rests on that very principle.

I didn't realize I was failing to take step one of this process myself. It's something I tell my clients to do for themselves all the time. Self-love. Self-compassion. Genuine self-acceptance, including acceptance of the body, here and now, the way it is.

I did not suffer from a lack of motivation to do this. Rather, I just couldn't see that an old way of looking at the world still shaped my mindset.

But now I am waking up. I glimpse that gap in myself between my ideals and my everyday living. A new paradigm was coming alive in me.

And in the process, *You Are Deathless* became a different book.

No longer was I trying to tell the story of a woman, me, who had cured herself of every ailment through the power of her mind. I discovered that this is not my story. For years I have been trying to shove my foot into Cinderella's glass slipper. But I'm not Cinderella or Wonder Woman—and for the first time, I do not want their fairytale lives. I have one, thank you very much, with its own triumphs and tribulations.

My story goes like this:

A woman, a real-life woman and not a character in a storybook, discovers, for real and not just in theory, that healing, and curing are not the same thing. She stops pushing herself to get better. She stops trying to prove herself. She even stops obsessing over finding a savior—religious, romantic, medical, or otherwise. Why? Because she doesn't need to be saved.

What she needs, a whole lot more than a white knight or a miracle cure, is gentleness. Tenderness. And she can give these things to herself, any old day of the week. Actually, she has learned that literally anyone has this same superpower. Few have developed it, though, and this makes her story, at the very least, helpful.

She does not live happily ever after. But she does live. She shows up for her life—this life, the one she has, not the one she wishes she had—with all the interest and gusto she can muster.

And this is not The End.

A Day in the Life

Stretch. Yawn. Blink, blink, stretch. I reach for the dark gray velvet drapes. Time to let in the light of day.

I stayed in my cozy four-poster bed this morning longer than I did yesterday. I'm not avoiding anything. Just listening. Because now I do that. I listen.

Body, what do you need today? I ask the question, then I listen.

On a physical level: Do you need a walk? A supplement? A medication? More water? Something else?

On an emotional level: Is there an emotion you need to process? Something triggered that you need to resolve.

Spiritually: Any messages for me?

I follow a daily meditation routine that grounds and nurtures me.

In a while I will be making breakfast, whatever I want, since Paul is already up and has fed himself and the dogs. I'll be doing it in a master-chef kitchen (the previous owner was a French chef) decorated to our tastes. After all the years of renting, I have thoroughly enjoyed creating a home together with my husband the way we both want it. Considering COVID, it represents no minor accomplishment, either. Even though we now live in the furniture capital of the US, most furniture is on backorder for months and brands of my childhood - Ethan Allen, Thompson, etc. have all closed. Thanks to lovely consignment stores in the area, though, we've found most everything we need, and I enjoy the feeling of reusing. I feel the coziness of the space wrap itself around me like a hug as I pour my first cup of coffee.

This time in the morning, when I gradually rouse myself and reconnect with the world—this is the best part of my day.

Of course, I also love my walks with the doggies. We usually go out twice a day. Passionately they sniff, nose, and investigate. They respond to most other dogs the same they do to cats—noisily. Seems they prefer the company of Paul, me, and one another. Sometimes the outing can last an hour when I stop to talk to neighbors. I have met so many people this way.

And I have discovered the joys of riding a bike, not pushing myself in a spin class to get my heart rate up and burn calories, obsessively. When I ride, I am not going somewhere. Rather, I ride for the sake of riding, pointing my handlebars in whatever direction suits my fancy. As a therapist once told me, take the pace of nature. I am finally taking her advice.

I suppose I do everything at a leisurely pace these days. For so many years I pushed my body hard. Even after I decided to leave my high-pressure job as the Wellness Director in Hawaii, I was still pressuring myself with building up my own private wellness consulting company. Always I needed to be... seeing more clients. How many? Well, just more than I already had, no matter that number. Also, I still needed to write a bestselling book. Oh, and become a famous inspirational speaker. Whatever I could actually do, here and now, could not possibly be enough.

All the while, I was ignoring my own needs. I operated on the notion that if I just used my mind well enough, I could push my body harder. Maybe someday it would toe the line.

Ha!

This week I don't even have any clients on my calendar. Not one. I might just take the day to snuggle with the dogs. I rest whenever I need it, sometimes two naps a day. I don't give myself grief about it, either. *It's about time*, I can hear my body say. Yes, it is.

You see, somewhere along the way I took on the notion of "living large." I'm not even sure now where I found the idea, but in my mind, I connect it with author, spiritual leader, and political activist, Marianne Williamson. For me to live large, I needed to have a big impact. I had to do "big things" like become famous and inspire the masses. I had to conquer all my frailties and become someone who "mattered." PS - that was not what she meant in her book *Return to Love*.

But in the last year, my definition of living large has changed entirely. I know now that it is my parent's definition combined with societal expectations.

No longer am I straining to live up to an idealized version of my life. Now living large means, to me, something as simple as sharing a lovely breakfast with Paul. Going for a long quiet walk with the dogs. Having a moment of creativity as I rearrange an area of my house. My life, this life that so many would call "little," has stretched to encompass the vastness of the cosmos. Living here, now, with loving kindness toward myself, looks to me like the largest life I can imagine.

Understand that I would love to be out there accomplishing stuff. I passionately believe in serving others, and I love the work I do. But I'm no longer willing to ignore what my body—or my heart, or my spirit, or my soul—truly needs.

And my new approach is working, too. Once I stopped pushing it, my body started improving. For one thing, the frequency of the migraines has gone down. When I get one, I take the medicine I need and rest—instead of railing at God and the universe and cursing my fate. I'm also working with my doctors to find ways to treat the PTSD. Before, I could not even admit to myself how much PTSD has ruled my life. Heck, I was only officially diagnosed with it two years ago. Now, I'm trying again with the meds the doctors recommend, to find a dose that works for me. I would love to go all natural, but I can see clearly how much my nervous system needs support to unwind and reset. Hopefully this treatment will help. If it doesn't, I'm sure I will find one that does. My intention for caring for myself and supporting my body has become so strong that I know I cannot fail.

My guides, my angels, my ancestors—they all walk with me. Throughout each day, I feel their love and support opening the path in front of me as I step onto it.

I am deathless – not physically, but as a soul. And I am finally starting to live like it.

Eye and I

Yesterday I got my North Carolina driver's license. I arrived at the DMV at the tail end of a migraine, not my best time for a photo. Inside, I sagged.

My photo showed it, too. The woman who took it kindly allowed me to see it before she printed it on my ID. I looked just as tired as I felt. Shoot.

Then I had a flash of inspiration.

"Wait, can we take that again?" I asked.

In the past I would have just lived with the terrible picture of myself, carrying it around everywhere and presenting it to strangers when asked. I would have accepted without question the notion that the weary-looking woman, clearly beset by troubles, was "me."

Now I was getting other ideas, though. I told myself, Nicole, you have the power to put yourself into a higher vibration at any minute, including right now. That's who you really are.

So, I did just that. Wow, what a difference.

"Boy, that is a big change!" the clerk said as she showed me the second photo. I had to agree. In the new photo, I could see the light, not just cast upon me by the flash, but blazing out from inside of me. My eyes shone.

"The eyes are the windows to the soul," the old saying goes. People have attributed this long-standing proverb to Cicero, to the Bible, to Shakespeare. In English, it has certainly been around in the form we know it since at least the mid-1500s. In other versions and languages, this wisdom has circulated since before the time of Christ. I suspect its endurance arises from its relevance. It touches something we know intuitively, without being taught.

I think of that night thirty-eight years ago. An evening when my own fate had teetered so precariously between life and death. At the scene of the accident, a single dilated eye pupil—mine—had grabbed John Hartling's attention. This alone, the last sparks of light in my right eye, had determined my fate.

Since then, I haven't seen many things. Sometimes because I couldn't, and other times because I simply didn't want to look. I have beaten myself up, blamed myself. In the wilderness I have wandered, forty years of trying to get other people to see me. My needs. My loneliness.

Before anyone could, though, I would have to begin to see myself.

This is how the accident and the corresponding NDE have forever changed me. To move forward from the crash, I had to die to an old way of living. I had to see my own soul. This eternal part of me did not need me to see it. Whether or not I recognized the fact, my soul was always weaving itself into and through every aspect of my existence. Still, my soul longed for me to receive the blessings of knowing myself as more than just this body. Time to wake up, it was saying to me. Time to open your eyes.

Recently I went back to 104 Banks Street in Jacksonville, NC, the little red house where my life began. Same color, same landscaping—not a thing had changed.

My home after my birth at Camp Lejeune Hospital, Easter, 1964.

Re-visiting where I started my life – 58 years later. Nothing much has changed. But I certainly have.

But I certainly have. I once got a second chance at my life (and a third). And it has caused me to see everything differently.

CHAPTER 12: NOT DONE DANCING

Lesson 12:

During a life review, we learn how everything we said, did, and thought during our physical life impacted ourselves, others, and the world.*

Minor, Major Miracles

As I complete the decades long process of writing this account the year is 2022. COVID is still with us in some form or another, along with yet another war, this one in Ukraine, my mother's birthplace.

I continue to live happily ever after with Paul, Beaux, and Bella in our new/old home in New Bern, NC. I feel an enormous sense of relief and accomplishment to finally put all this in print. And I feel anxiety: How will this book be received by the public? By my family? By others who are described here?

I have started and stopped writing countless times in the several decades of this process. It was often excruciating to revisit events I had buried, and my body let me know emphatically when my spirit had had enough. Yet I kept coming back to this writing, to myself. And ultimately, it has been cathartic and healing. So, I hope that this text which I composed for myself can also offer some insights and light to others as well. It holds my truth, my purpose, my self.

---

* Source: https://mcusercontent.com/6aeb61681f6c311e999fff730/files/5070a118-63b3-4ac3-87f4-08b4f5d6e2e0/2020_IANDS_Annual_Report.01.pdf pg. 15

Messed Up

Messed up! That day I woke up in the ICU thirty-nine years ago, I used those words inside my head to remake my whole identity. So many terrible things had happened to my body. It would always be weak. With so much trauma and scarring, I could never hope to be healthy again or lead a normal life. I would always suffer. Even though I found myself awake in a hospital bed, I had entered an emotional coma.

As a kid I had believed in the power of God to heal me. I knew God could do anything. But then the accident happened. Nothing had panned out the way the grownups had taught me it would. Sure, maybe those angels had put me back in my body, but then they had ditched me. God had abandoned me to a life of pain and suffering.

I had given up on God altogether. If I was going to get through life, either I had to do it myself or get someone else who would do it for me.

But after my session with Julie, I started to grasp that healing, true healing, comes from Spirit alone. Nothing from the outside, no matter how many times a day I drink it, do it, or slather it onto my body, it can ever initiate lasting transformation. Miracles arise from the inside, from the Soul, from God, and work their way outward into the physical plane.

Here's what I mean.

Around Thanksgiving of 2021, I found myself dealing with a migraine. So inconvenient. Paul's family had come, a visit I had been looking forward to for months. Now here I was, two days in bed.

I had already gone through my new routine of questions. What do you need physically, Nicole? More Imitrex, came the answer. But it didn't help. Then I asked, what do you need emotionally? With this, I followed my guidance to do some NET work. I experienced an emotional shift, but the headache was still there. Then I asked, does this migraine call for spiritual healing?

Yes! The answer came swiftly and clearly.

With this, I reflected on all the times I was healed against all odds. Case in point, I had survived the car accident and months in the hospital. Then I visualized myself as healed, and I truly believed it. I started acting that way, too. Instead of talking about what was wrong with me, I was focusing on all that was right. When I filled out a new physician's intake form, I even felt disconnected from anything I could put in the "wrong" categories. Just writing about it felt off to me.

Then I laid down to rest. As I was drifting to sleep, I heard a voice. Deep and resonant, the voice seemed to come from somewhere far away.

"Nicole, your faith has made you well."

Was I imagining things? For a while now I've been working with my guides and angels. But I've never experienced anything like this voice. It held such power. More than a statement, it seemed to be making a command.

This must be the voice of God, I told myself.

At the sound of that voice, I got out of bed at 10:46 a.m. At noon, I walked with Paul to a nearby restaurant, where we ate a delightful lunch with his family. What's more, I did everything else we had planned, the whole Thanksgiving weekend from start to finish. For the remainder of the holiday the headache did not return.

I went three weeks without a migraine. Maybe it doesn't sound like much. But I haven't gone this long without one in three decades.

And here's the deal. This healing is something I did not "do," at least not in the sense we usually use that word. I had not made an effort to heal.

For quite a while now I have been connecting every day to my guides and angels. I have visualized myself feeling better and better. I am also learning more all the time about how to work with energy for healing. So, you can say I've spent a lot of time priming the pump.

The actual healing, though, did not come from me. That voice I heard was not emanating from inside my head. God, the Holy Spirit, the Great I Am. Use the name you prefer. The highest part of me partnered with my soul and personality to activate greater well-being in my physical body.

What a relief I've experienced from discovering that healing does not rest on my shoulders alone. The more I try to control it, in fact, the less room it has to enter my life. I do my work, yes. I show up. I'd say that's only about 10 percent of the equation, though. God does the rest.

All these years I had it backwards. I went looking outside myself for a cure. I started with a degree in nutrition. When that didn't change things for me, I pursued emotional healing. Now I find myself returning to the spiritual—the Source of wellness.

For decades since I left my public health position at the CDC in 2003, I have worked in the field of prevention and wellness. Whether as a project manager for kid's health, an oncology dietitian, vice-president at the American Cancer Society-Pacific Division, and even going back to work at the Air Force Medical Operations in San Antonio, TX as their health promotion nutrition manager for all seventy-eight bases worldwide, I have touched jobs in all sectors - private, non-profit, academia, clinical, military, etc. The AF consultant gig, well, that was truly coming full circle, as I experienced what I would have done had I stayed in the military. Finally serving as the wellness director of a hospital that was Christian based, I really got it, wellness rarely focuses on the emotional or spiritual. Most of us treat it like an afterthought. Yet it can have the greatest impact on our well-being. Perhaps the story of my own life, not just this anecdote of a cured headache, but the whole of it, including my experiences beyond the body and my body's return from death against all odds, presents the best evidence I can give on the healing power of Spirit.

Life truly is a circular journey moving through our issues and tissues. It is also why, whenever we work to release a habit, change a pattern, or overcome a fear, we often encounter that issue one last time, even after we thought we had conquered it. Kind of like an examination. The reappearance of a pattern, habit, or fear is often a sign that we have come full circle, and that if we can maintain our resolve through one last test, we will achieve a new level of mastery in our lives.

My Life Review

I had an abbreviated life review, I suppose, since I was so young when I had my car accident. Plus, I did not stay dead for very long. What I can tell you is that up till then, my soul was on the wrong path. I had never individuated as a youngster and did everything I was told to do for fear of being punished. I was living in fear, pleasing all others to my own detriment, got "God " wrong with believing I was going to hell and was a sinner, believing unconsciously, at my core, I was unlovable. There is the root belief system. I would never become the person I was created to be while living from these beliefs. I needed to come back to break free of these harmful, painful, and downright wrong belief systems.

Why did I write this book?

"There are years that ask questions and years that answer."
- Zora Neale Hurston

You may remember that the beings I encountered beyond death told me to share their message, "You do not need to fear death."

This assignment first sparked my desire to put pen to paper. I wanted to write a book for anyone who needed to hear that truth which I had experienced firsthand. I was writing the book for you.

How surprised I was to discover along the way that I was also writing the book for myself. I, too, needed to hear the message of my angels, in my own voice. I have needed to discover the many nuances of meaning that this message holds, not just for others, but for me.

So, thank you. Thank you for being a willing participant with me in the unfolding journey we are taking together.

May this book help you with your fears about death. Haven't we all experienced firsthand that with every ending comes a new beginning? I have seen what awaits you at the end of this life. I can assure you, it's a new beginning more beautiful than you can comprehend. Anita Moorjini reminds us in her book, *What If This Is Heaven*?. "When we die, we will be able to see the whole picture of our life at one glance, understanding why events and circumstances happened the way they did and WHY we made the choices we made."

May this book also support you through the loss of loved ones. Nothing I can say will take away the grief that comes from a loved one's transition from this realm to the next one. Yet I hope you will find some solace in knowing those you care for have not ceased to be. Rather, they continue onward, into the next great adventure, and they are waiting for you.

And above all, may my book inspire you to live. Fully, freely, with your heart and your hands as open as you can make them. I'm not talking about a life of constant unicorns and rainbows here. Only in fairy tales can you find a life without scars or pain. But this life, the one you have, where you are as you are, right now, has in it everything you ever really wanted. I hope my words can in some small way help you find inside yourself what you've always been seeking.

Take a good look at your soul and you will see: You are deathless.

EPILOGUE

Revelations

It is summer of 2022 and this book is complete. My former roommates from the AFA and I planned a Zoom call to catch-up. Nicole had initiated the call and we all agreed. I had stayed in touch with two of these women over the years, but one, Margaret, none of us had heard from since my accident. We did not know what she was doing, where she was living, or anything about her life other than what she shared with friends on Facebook. We were excited to "see" her and catch up with one another.

That excitement quickly turned to confusion, frustration, sadness, and so many other emotions. Margaret revealed to us the truth of what had happened the night of my accident. Margaret was supposed to have taken me home that evening. She had been my planned ride (I *had* made a safe and logical plan, something I did not remember and had beat myself up for all these years). Nicole, why did you not have a safe plan to get home? Why did you agree to get in the car with Nate? You know that was stupid and unsafe! I hear my parents' voices saying these same things to me. We all knew I made a bad decision that night, and because of that decision I was going to suffer, maybe even the rest of my life. Right?

Margaret explained that there was another upper-class cadet there that evening that she had a crush on. Since he was drunk, she offered to drive his car back to the Academy. When I asked her for a ride back to the Academy she said, "No, I want to be alone with him." She told me there was another upperclassman I could get a ride with. I told her that he had been drinking. She stated, "Well, they all have been drinking. Just go, you will be alright." Little did she know we would wind up stopping at a bar, stopping to see the sun set, and never make it back to the Academy. I went with it and tried to have fun. One "fun" night that forever changed my life and hers.

Margaret told us of how she had lived with extreme guilt ever since my accident and that this was why she had dropped out of the AFA. She could "not imagine being at the Academy without Nicole." She left the AFA during the Christmas break and was never seen or heard from again. To us, her former roommates, it was as though she had fallen off the face of the earth. We never heard from her again, had no idea if she married, what she did for a living, or anything about her life. She literally disappeared.

She confessed that she blamed herself for everything that had happened to me and all I had suffered. It still haunts her today. She said she lived her life constantly wondering, what if? What if she had not told me to ride with Nate and just drove me back? So many what ifs.

She had suffered as much as me but in a very different way. But during our call she had felt the need to speak her truth, apologize, and ask for my forgiveness. At the end of the day, it is very sad, and the truth is we were both victims.

When I heard this confession, I went into a state of shock and disassociation. I could not believe what I was hearing and that she held on to this truth for thirty-eight years. My body's response was a migraine that lasted eight days after which I finally had to go to the ER and be knocked out with a med cocktail. Obviously, I needed time to process all of this but first I had to take care of myself and allow my body to process this revelation and how it impacts me, spiritually, physically, and emotionally.

I am grateful for Margaret's revelation and to have the final pieces of the puzzle fit together. I did not have another option for a ride back to the Academy as we were the last to leave. I did confront her about why she didn't say anything earlier. She thought I remembered our conversation from that fateful evening.

A friend and I were recently discussing how he had been carrying self-blame for things that happened a LONG time ago, so he totally understood why she felt that way. It also reminded him of a time when he apologized to someone for something from many years ago, and the person said, "Well thanks, but I don't even remember that happening."

Amazing how much pain we can cause ourselves, isn't it???

As with all healing, this will take work and time. I am certain this information was revealed at the perfect time but WHOA! Two months before publication another bomb of healing dropped!

Doolie roommates, Lori, Nicole, Sharon, and Margaret after a Saturday morning parade. We would not have made it without one another! A super glue bonding experience.

Driver of the Car (Nate Smith)

People almost always ask me, "What happened to the driver?" So, to wrap things up, here is what I know. Nate was taken to a separate hospital for treatment of injuries and was back at the Academy after a week. He was able to rejoin his sports team and graduate in May 1984. I saw Nate when I went back for more surgery in 1984, and to attend graduation and visit with my classmates. It was a brief interaction, but he said to me that since I was walking everything was okay. Clearly that was not the case, and you can NEVER judge someone strictly by their apparent physical functioning!

When I was in cognitive behavioral therapy in 2001, my therapist suggested I write an angry letter to Nate. Being a compliant client, I streamed four pages worth (this was before my memory of the crash came back). Later that month I received a letter from him and much to my disappointment he was defensive and claimed he had apologized in front of my two roommates during that interaction in June of 1984 (which he did not). Nate said he had moved on and hoped I would too. My therapist was shocked that I had mailed the letter and that he responded. I have not seen or spoken to him since.

My Siblings' Reactions

Sean

My youngest brother, Sean, who was in the 8th grade at the time of the crash was away at the Marine Military Academy:

> *"The shock of it all. The disbelief that it had actually happened. The fact that I was completely unaware of Nicole's situation and the severity of her injuries. The realization that I could have lost my sister and been none the wiser until my family decided I should be told remains unsettling to this day. I was the only family member that did not visit Nicole in Colorado. I still do not fully understand this decision by our parents, especially in the period immediately following the incident when Nicole's very survival was uncertain.*
>
> *"I am blessed and thankful that Nicole survived. We have always enjoyed a special relationship—she has always looked after her baby brother. One of my favorite photos is of her holding a very young me in the swimming pool—she wouldn't let anything happen to me.*
>
> *"I choose to believe that my parents made the best decisions possible when dealing with the very complex situation they were presented with. Doesn't make the results any easier to manage and how I felt marginalized, however, I do not begrudge them of the way they handled every parent's worst nightmare."*

James

My brother, James, who was a freshman at Louisiana State University at the time of the accident:

> *"Upon hearing of Nicole's accident, I was overcome with a sense of disbelief. I wanted nothing more for her than to simply survive."*

James flew out to see me approximately eight weeks after the crash when I was in the Pediatric Unit.

> *"When I saw you in the PEDS Unit, I was praying that you would make it through. I had never seen you in this condition, so it was very confronting. I tried to be encouraging and lift your Spirit as much as humanly possible"*

Note: The one thing I remember from his visit is that he came when my dinner was being served and it was fish. I was not eating much so to encourage me he took a bite and said how yummy it was—better than fried catfish. So, I ate a couple of bites and thought, "This is the worst tasting fish I have ever eaten." Years later, he told me he almost gagged getting it down. He was trying to be supportive.

Rachel

My sister, Rachel, was a senior at Southern Methodist University at the time of the accident.

> *"I was the one the AFA was finally able to get through to the night of the crash. (My parents were traveling.) All they told me was that she was in a car crash and hospitalized and to try and get word to my parents. So I called our neighbor and friend, Carolyn, and she kept trying to reach them at home until 1:00 am when she finally reached them. My dad called me later in the week and said he was going to see Nicole and would stop-over in Dallas to pick me up. I saw Nicole in the ICU and was mortified that this was my sister. I barely recognized her. I then went to the hospital Nate was in. When I walked in his room, he was sitting up in bed smoking a cigarette. I was beyond furious and let him have it. My sister is fighting for her life and your arrogant self is smoking away. I was very distressed that entire semester, even failing a class. I never knew when the phone rang if it would be to tell me she had passed away."*

Enjoying a rare moment in 2018 of us siblings together. We even did a round of Bible Drill! James won. (L to R: James, Nicole, Rachel and Sean)

Angel Updates, Where Are They Now?

I have often been asked about my team of angels, the unique heroes who pulled me through the horrors of my injuries. Here is the latest update as of 2022.

Amilu Stewart, MD (retired)

I had the opportunity to meet with Dr. Stewart in March of 2017 while attending a health promotion conference at The Broadmoor Hotel in Colorado Springs. We met for coffee, conversation, health news, of course, and her retirement news.

In 2008, at the age of seventy, Dr. Stewart retired after forty-five years of practice. Today, at age eighty-five, she remains active on the admissions committee at the University of Colorado Health Sciences Center, in her church, and of course with her family. In 2011, fifty years after Jefferson accepted female students, they bestowed upon her the Distinguished Alumni Award. In 2021, she published, *Breaking Barriers: The Story of Dr. Amilu Stewart*, which she wrote in 2011.

Catching up in 2017 at The Broadmoor Hotel in Colorado Springs – more coffee!

John Hartling, EMT (retired)

When I sent part of the manuscript to John for fact checking, he responded:

> *"I broke down in tears several times as I read it and had a hard time reading as the tears ran down my face.*
>
> *"You brought back lots of memories of my own near-death experiences. I've had over twenty surgeries, including having half my stomach removed and a pancreatic tumor. I was given a fifty-fifty chance of surviving both of these and even surviving the surgery itself. But here I am at eighty, still a hard-ass (probably an accurate description) and old and ugly! I go to Catholic Mass every morning to praise and thank God, go to the gym to lift weights, and then go home to annoy Karen (my wife), but life is good."*

Enjoying an evening in 2008 with John in Colorado Springs.

Pat Hartling, Paramedic (retired)

Remember the sixteen-year-old kid that accompanied his dad as part of the junior volunteer program to the scene of my crash? Well, I got to meet Pat and spend Christmas 2018 with him in Hawaii. Pat was there with his girlfriend and the elevator in the high-rise hotel they were staying in lost power. After walking up and down to and from the fourteenth floor twice, they called me to share their situation. Naturally, we invited them to come and stay with us. They spent the remainder of their vacation at our Kailua home, hanging at the beach! Pat retired after thirty-six years as a paramedic in Colorado and now resides in Florida. See, life does come full circle in so many ways.

Pat and I met for the first time since he saw me "dead." His first recovery experience as a junior volunteer. What a Christmas gift!

Sandy Haugen, RN (retired)

Sandy finally retired. She worked the first sixteen months of the pandemic. In 1988 she changed positions to PACU (recovery room). For thirty-three years, PACU was her last specialty. Her four children are all married with children. She has nine grandchildren. At age fifty-nine, she realized she didn't have a hobby, so she started competing in horse competitions. Now her calendar is full of everything she has chosen for the day.

Sandy, realizing we were almost the same height - she had not seen me upright!

Jan Williamson, USAF Captain, (retired)

Retired and living the dream in Arizona! We had the opportunity to meet on a regular basis in Hawaii when she came to stay at Bellows AFB on the Windward side for vacation!

Are we happy to see each other?

My Parents, Erika and James Kerr

My parents, both eighty-four, are in good health, and live outside of Melbourne, Australia. We have a family business Red Roo Sales and Service in which my father is still active. Both my parents are active in two churches, ministering and being of service to the Lord.

I did share with them the revelation of my roommate and what the truth really was, that Nate was the only ride left. I knew before he even said it, "Well, it was still a bad decision, and you should have walked back to the Academy."

Last visit with my parents, James and Erika, in Melbourne, Australia, April 2019.

Paul Deering, PhD

My soulmate and rockstar hubby, Paul! I could not have made it this far without you, my love!

Paul retired in June 2020 from being Professor of Education at the University of Hawaii. His career spanned forty-two years in education, including nine years of middle school teaching. Since making the move to New Bern, Paul's music career has been booming. Check him out at Doctor Paul Songwriter on YouTube. Paul stays busy with home improvements, doggie business, volunteering with Habitat for Humanity, politics, and of course ME! Married eighteen years, his longest ever. Life this amazing still catches him by surprise.

Falcons

I also want to give a shout out to the AFA football team from 1983, the Falcons, and their head coach, Ken Hatfield, for dedicating the AFA vs. Wyoming game to me.

AFA-7, Wyoming-14.

RESOURCES

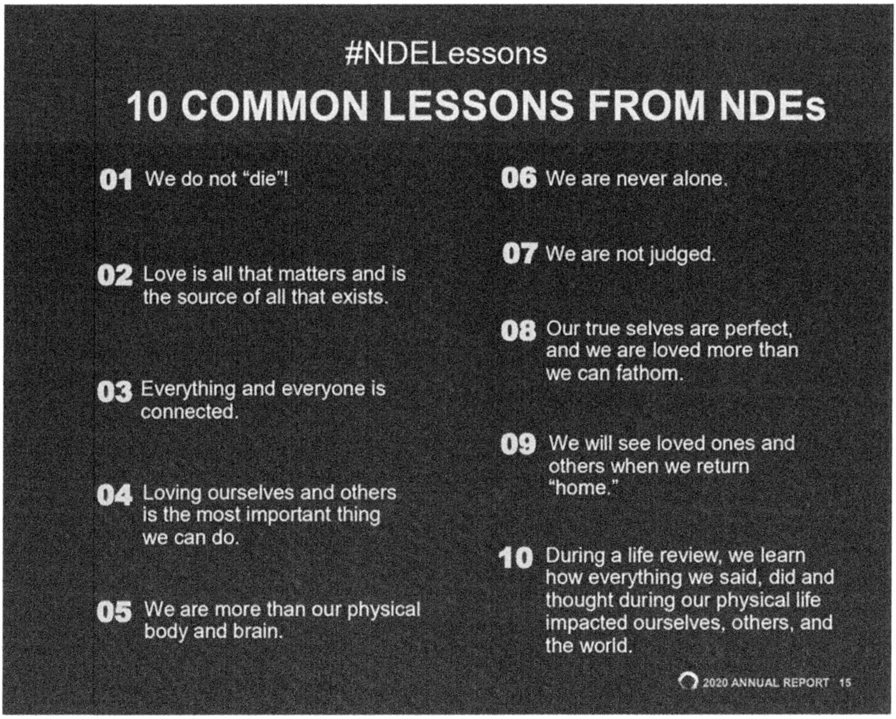

Neuro Emotional Technique

If you would like to know more about Neuro Emotional Technique (NET) and/or find a practitioner close to you please visit: https://www.netmindbody.com

ABOUT NICOLE

Award-winning health expert Nicole Kerr is the co-author of *Eating the Rainbow: Lifelong Nutritional Wellness—Without Lies, Hype, or Calculus*. She has appeared on CNN, PBS, CBS, ABC, the Food Channel, and a host of other TV and radio shows to share her unique perspective on wellness, lifestyle, and nutrition.

For the past thirty years, Nicole has worked in all sectors of society, including in government (the Centers for Disease Control and Prevention), non-profit (American Cancer Society), military (United States Air Force Medical Operations), academia (University of Hawaii), healthcare institutions/hospitals (Adventist Health Castle and Queens Medical Center), corporate settings (Sea Ties, LLC), and private consultation. Nicole's warm, engaging presentations have earned her a place in front of international audiences ranging from corporate food producers to health and medical associations. Throughout her career, she has focused on supporting people from every walk of life to make realistic, meaningful, happy choices for lifelong health and well-being.

When she was a nineteen-year-old cadet at the United States Air Force Academy, Nicole would be forced to learn how to live and love differently following a terrifying and transformative Near-Death Experience. Her memory of the crash came back twenty years later, and it has taken Nicole almost another two decades to align her soul, spirit, mind, and body, proving healing is certainly a non-linear process.

A disabled veteran, Nicole now maintains a private practice primarily using Neuro Emotional Technique (NET) targeting the often-overlooked domains of emotional, energy, and spiritual well-being.

~

"Don't be afraid of death" is my call to action which was made very clear to me when my memory returned. How to do that started with writing this book decades ago. I am grateful, deeply grateful, for the opportunity to share it all with you. I now count you among the many loving people who have helped me find my way through the many challenges the crash created for me.

For media inquiries, public speaking, and to continue to connect with Nicole on her journey, visit her at www.NicoleKerr.com.

AUTHOR SUGGESTED BOOK CLUB QUESTIONS

Nicole Angelique's Note:

Death is a heavy topic for most people. The 10 Common Lessons from NDE's are the main take-a-ways from this book in regards to resolving your fears around death. Notice, they are ALL positive! Based on my NDE experience I am now on a journey to help, as Dr. William Bloom states, "...to magic away death's gloom and doom. I want everyone at every age to understand the cosmic context. Please do not misunderstand me. There is still suffering, grief, pain, loss, and poignancy that we must carefully and compassionately hold and heal. But the cosmic context is benevolent and extraordinary. Knowing the true context enables us to live a happier life, to prepare for our own graceful passing, and also to support others as they approach their own transition."

Also, I cannot say enough about emotional healing. We all have emotions we have pushed or stuffed down during our lives. When we feel, we heal. The word heal has a common origin with the words whole and holy, pointing to a relationship of body to spirit. Enjoy your discussion!

1. How was the emotional experience of reading this book for you? How are you feeling about what Nicole experienced? (Note: If these questions do not resonate with you, how can you interact with your emotions and body to get them free and flowing?)
2. Do you believe "we are deathless – we do not 'die'? Did this book help change your mind in any way on this point?
3. Nicole goes into some length about how ascribed identities can cause us to "die." Her biggest one was being a people-pleaser. What identities do you define yourself by that are harming you now? *(Internalized versions of God are a good place for people to look for built-in identities, where they have been trapped in a physiological response to things.* This is a big area where the unconscious mind is functioning.)

4. What is your concept of God? How is this playing into your fear of death? Consider a few ways in which your image of your father may have affected your perception of God, which in turn affects your self-image. If your father was distant, impersonal and uncaring, and he wouldn't intervene for you, you may see God as having the same characteristics. As a result, you may feel that you are unworthy of God's intervention in your life. You find it difficult to draw close to God because you see Him as disinterested in your needs and wants. If your father was like a drill sergeant, demanding more and more from you with no expression of satisfaction, or burning with anger with no tolerance for mistakes, you may have cast God in his image. You likely feel God will not accept you unless you meet His demands, which seem unattainable. This perception may have driven you to become a perfectionist.
5. Do you believe you are never alone? Why or why not? (Note: There is a difference between alone and lonely.) Are you at peace dying without any physical person around you? Why or why not?
6. If you really believed we are not judged by God/Source how would you live your life differently?
7. Trauma (especially given the COVID pandemic) is endemic in the world. If you choose to heal your trauma wounds it is not a linear or easy task. However, the reward of finally coming to love self and others is the most important thing we can do. Do you have trauma wounds you have not addressed? If so, what can you do to begin on a path towards healing?
8. What do you imagine will happen at death? Does knowing that you will see loved ones and others when we return "home" bring you peace?
9. Do you believe in angels/guides? If so, do you ask them for help? If you believe in them and do not ask for help, why not?
10. How can you start changing the ways you act and words you use around death to be more positive and enlightening?

Finally, If anyone in the group has experienced an NDE and they feel like sharing their experience, please do.

What fears do you experience when you think about your own death?

Check All That Apply

- ❒ I worry what will happen to me after death.
- ❒ I am anxious about the way I will die.
- ❒ I wonder whether I will die with dignity.
- ❒ I fear the physical pain of dying.
- ❒ I don't want to leave my family alone.
- ❒ I worry I haven't fulfilled my life's purpose.
- ❒ I worry about my lack of control over how and when I will die.
- ❒ I fear ceasing to exist.
- ❒ I worry about not having a legacy.
- ❒ I worry about all the things I'll miss after I die.
- ❒ I dream a lot about dying.
- ❒ I suffer from past unresolved trauma. (i.e. parent or child dying)
- ❒ I fear dying alone.
- ❒ Other fears?

Printed in Great Britain
by Amazon

25829137R00106